Melissa Stock is a barrister at Normanton Chambers practising in data, privacy and information law. She advises and represents individuals, companies, public bodies and non-governmental organisations in all areas of privacy and data protection. Melissa also advises on data governance issues and the use of data more broadly in a policy and international context. She writes a blog and produces podcasts:

www.privacylawbarrister.com.

The Right to be Forgotten
The Law and Practical Issues

The Right to be Forgotten
The Law and Practical Issues

Melissa Stock
Barrister, Lincoln's Inn
MA BA (Hons)

Law Brief Publishing

Published 2020 by Law Brief Publishing, an imprint of Law Brief Publishing Ltd
30 The Parks
Minehead
Somerset
TA24 8BT

www.lawbriefpublishing.com

Paperback: 978-1-912687-81-7

To my family, for all their love and patience.

PREFACE

This book is for legal practitioners, privacy professionals, data protection officers, organisations that handle personal data and anyone interested in the law that governs the control of personal information, in particular the aspect of erasure.

The different components that make up the right to be forgotten are explained and key questions answered, such as the legal basis for making erasure requests, and the possible exemptions from complying. The judgment that established the right to be forgotten is examined in detail, as well as some important cases that have followed.

The law stated in this book is believed to be correct and up-to-date at 30th September 2020.

Melissa Stock
September 2020

CONTENTS

CHAPTER I
INTRODUCTION

The so-called 'right to be forgotten' case led to a seminal judgment from the Court of Justice of the European Union ('CJEU') in privacy and data protection.[1] The 2014 ruling attracted much criticism,[2] but the concept was not new. The 'right to be forgotten' had already been considered in certain Member States[3] and was included in the proposal for a 'General Data Protection Regulation' in 2012.[4] In 2016, the General Data Protection Regulation (EU) 2016/679 on the protection of natural persons with regard to the processing of personal data and the free movement of such data ('GDPR') was introduced, and came into force on 25 May 2018.

The purpose of the GDPR is to bring data protection legislation in Europe up to date with the extraordinary advances in technology and the changes in the way society uses data. It replaced Directive 95/46/EC[5] (the 'Data Protection Directive'), which was enacted before the ad-

---

1   *Google Spain SL, Google Inc. v Agencia Española de Protección de Datos (AEPD), Mario Costeja González, Court of Justice (Grand Chamber), Case C-131/12,* 13 May 2014, ECLI:EU:C:2014:317.

2   See for example K Byrum, 'The European Right to be Forgotten: The First Amendment Enemy' Lexington, 2018; Jeffrey Rosen, 'The Right to be Forgotten' (2012) 64 Stanford Law Review Online 88.

3   For example, in 2009, the French Secretary of State for the digital economy initiated a campaign the *'Chartre Du Droit a l'Oubli Dan Les Sites Collaboratifs et Les Moteurs de Recherche'* to introduce a code of practice related to the right to be forgotten on social media and search engines.

4   'Proposal for a regulation of the European Parliament and of the Council on the protection of individuals with regard to the processing of personal data and on the free movement of such data (General Data Protection Regulation) COM (2012) 11 final', 25 January 2012.

5   'Of the European Parliament and of the Council of 24 October 1995 on the protection of individuals with regard to the processing of personal data and on

vent of technologies and communication methods such as social media networks, smart phones, internet search engines, Google maps, facial recognition technology, the internet of things, drones, and voice recognition applications. The GDPR places an emphasis on data subject rights, increases obligations of controllers of personal data and has introduced new concepts that were absent from the Data Protection Directive such as 'profiling', 'pseudonymisation' and 'data protection by design and default'.[6]

The massive expansion of data creation and the 'datafication' of our everyday lives has led to growing concerns that individuals no longer have effective control over their personal data.[7] The ease with which it is now possible to access, copy, re-use and publish information on the internet, whilst bringing enormous opportunity, has also made it increasingly difficult to control the information that is available about ourselves. The increasing use of online resources and platforms, whilst connecting us globally and making services cheap and efficient, has also unfortunately led to the misuse of data such that it can have serious consequences. The Cambridge Analytica scandal exposed the scale of the problem of the lack of transparency in the use of our personal data, the extent of profiling, and the potential it has to threaten our democratic system.[8]

Whilst the right to be forgotten has been criticised as an affront to the right to freedom of expression, this overlooks the plethora of very real problems that the existence of information on the internet can pose to individuals, some of which are especially damaging and include, for example:

---

the free movement of such data'.

6   These concepts are touched upon in Chapters IV and V.

7   See European Commission Impact Assessment SEC (2012) 72 final, 25 January 2012, paragraph 3.6.2.

8   See the House of Commons Digital, Culture, Media and Sport Committee, 'Disinformation and 'fake news': Interim Report', 24 July 2018.

- Identity theft;

- Fraud;

- Refusal or loss of employment[9];

- Refusal of educational entry;

- Online harassment and bullying[10]; and in extreme cases,

- Suicide and self-harm.[11]

According to the European Commission, strengthening the right to be forgotten in the GDPR will help individuals to manage their online data protection risks and is about *'empowering people, not about erasing past events, re-writing history or restricting freedom of the press'.*[12] A

---

9   Often cited is the case of Ashley Payne, a U.S. schoolteacher who was forced to resign because of photos on her Facebook page, showing her drinking alcohol with a caption that included an expletive: *Payne v Barrow County School District (2009) Civil Case No 09CV-3038-X (Super.Ct.Ga.)*.

10 The case of Christos Catsouras is a shocking example. The family were harassed online after images of their daughter's body, who had died in a car accident, were placed on the internet: *Christos Catsouras et al v Department of California Highway Patrol 181 Cal.App 4th 856 (2010)*. See also the so-called 'Gamergate' scandal, where a harassment campaign was initiated against several women in the video game industry, including Zoe Quinn, which was sparked by a blogpost written by her ex-boyfriend: Quinn, Zoë, 'Crash Override: How Gamergate (Nearly) Destroyed My Life, and How We Can Win the Fight Against Online Hate', Public Affairs, 5 September 2017.

11 The tragic examples of Molly Russell in the United Kingdom, who killed herself after viewing self-harm content on Instagram. See the family's campaign: https://www.leighday.co.uk/News/2019/January-2019/Family-of-Molly-Russell-call-for-greater-protectio; and Amanda Todd in the United States, who suffered relentless abuse after the repeated posting of an intimate photograph online that led to her suicide. See the official site, the Amanda Todd Legacy: https://www.amandatoddlegacy.org/about-amanda.html

12 'How will the data protection reform affect social networks' European Commission, January 2016.

Eurobarometer Special Survey found that the majority of Europeans are uneasy about the everyday disclosure of their personal data, which is necessary to make purchases or access services.[13] Social media has become particularly problematic, especially in the context of young persons, who as they enter adulthood may no longer want information and photographs that have been uploaded either by themselves or others, made available to the public.

The right to be forgotten is commonly understood and used in the context of privacy and reputation. However, it in fact encompasses the right to object to personal data use, the right to erasure and the right to be delisted from search engine results. In Chapter II, I shall evaluate the relationship between privacy and data protection.

In the right to be forgotten judgment ('*Google Spain*'), the CJEU did not explicitly use the phrase 'the right to be forgotten', although the wording was included in submissions to the court. The GDPR incorporates the outcome of *Google Spain*. Article 17 of the GDPR is labelled the 'Right to erasure' with the 'right to be forgotten' added afterwards in parentheses. Article 17 of the GDPR gives an individual the right to have their personal data deleted, but only under a set of specific circumstances.

Chapter III sets out the fundamental data protection concepts in the GDPR and I shall explain Article 17 in more depth, including its relationship with the 'right to object'. The right to be forgotten in the Data Protection Act 2018 is also reviewed in the chapter.

The *Google Spain* right to be forgotten judgment is summarised in Chapter IV. The term 'right to be delisted' is used by the European Data Protection Board ('EDPB') to describe when GDPR Article 17 is applied to search engine operators (as was the case in the *Google Spain*

---

13 Special Eurobarometer 431 – Data Protection, June 2015.

ruling). The EDPB has issued guidance on delisting, which will be explored in Chapter V.

In Chapter VI, I shall outline some practical issues that may arise for individuals and organisations when making or receiving erasure requests; I also highlight some particular topics of interest such as metadata and anonymisation. A review of some important right to be forgotten cases in the courts since the *Google Spain* judgment is set out in Chapter VII, and Chapter VIII will address remedies and appeals. An overview of the position in the United Kingdom (UK) after Brexit is found in Chapter IX.

CHAPTER II
PRIVACY AND DATA PROTECTION

The 'right to privacy' and the 'right to data protection' have been given equal importance by the Charter of Fundamental Rights of the European Union ('the Charter') and yet the relationship between privacy and data protection is not straightforward. Prior to the incorporation of the Charter into Union law as part of the Treaty of Lisbon in 2009, the CJEU cited the provisions of the European Convention on Human Rights ('the Convention') when interpreting the Data Protection Directive in relation to fundamental rights.

Article 7 of the Charter, 'Respect for Private and Family Life', provides that *'everyone has the right to respect for his or her private and family life, home and communications'*. The wording reflects, in part, Article 8 of the Convention, which is as follows:

> '1.   *Everyone has the right to respect for his private and family life, his home and his correspondence.*
>
> 2.   *There shall be no interference by a public authority with the exercise of this right except such as is in accordance with the law and is necessary in a democratic society in the interests of national security, public safety or the economic well-being of the country, for the prevention of disorder or crime, for the protection of health or morals, or for the protection of the rights and freedoms of others.'*

The close connection between Article 7 of the Charter and Article 8 of the Convention was highlighted by the CJEU in *Volker und Markus*

Schecke GbR and Hartmut Eifert v Land Hessen.[1] However, it is important to note that there are differences in the way that private life is interpreted by the European Court of Human Rights ('ECtHR') and the CJEU in respect to data protection, in part because of the requirement of finding 'necessity' in Article 8(2) of the Convention. The ECtHR has also held that data protection is capable of engaging both Article 8 of the Convention and Article 10 of the Convention ('the right to freedom of expression'),[2] whilst Article 7 and 8 in the Charter are distinct rights.

Article 8 of the Charter, 'Protection of Personal Data', provides as follows:

> *'8(1): Everyone has the right to the protection of personal data concerning him or her.*
>
> *8(2): Such data must be processed fairly for specified purposes and on the basis of the consent of the person concerned or some other legitimate basis laid down by law. Everyone has the right of access to data which has been collected concerning him or her, and the right to have it rectified.*
>
> *8(3): Compliance with these rules shall be subject to control by an independent authority.'*

There is a growing body of case law in the CJEU referring to the right to data protection provided by Article 8 of the Charter. Examples include:

---

1   *CJEU Cases C-468/10 and C-469/10,* 9 November 2010, ECLI:EU:C:2010:662, at paragraph 47.

2   See the cases *McMichael v UK (1995) 20 EHRR 205* and *Társaság a Szabadságjogokért v. Hungary*, application no. 37374/05, 14 April 2009.

- Fingerprints and passports – *Michael Schwarz v Stadt Bochum, Case C-291/12, 17 October 2013.*[3]

- Electronic communications – *Digital Rights Ireland Ltd v Ireland, Case C-293/12 and Case C-594-12, 8 April 2014.*[4]

- Social media data – *Maximillian Schrems v Data Protection Commissioner Case C-362/14, 6 October 2015*[5]; *Data Protection Commissioner v Facebook Ireland Limited, Maximillian Schrems Case C-311/18, 16 July 2020.*[6]

- Door-to-door data collection – *Tietosuojavaltuutettu v Jehovan todistajat – uskonnollinen yhdyskunta, Case C-25/17, 10 July 2018.*[7]

- 'YouTube' postings – *Sergejs Buivids v. Datu valsts inspekcija, Case C-345/17, 14 February 2019.*[8]

- Directories – *Deutsche Telekom AG v Bundesrepublik Deutschland, Case C-543/09, 5 May 2011.*[9]

Despite the fact that privacy and data protection are defined as two separate rights in the Charter, the jurisprudence of Europe's highest courts has considered there to be an interrelationship between privacy and data protection. The CJEU has interpreted the scope of private life as including the protection of personal data: *'it must be considered that the right to respect for private life with regard to the processing of personal data, recognised by Articles 7 and 8 of the Charter, concerns any information relating to an identified or identifiable individual and the limitations which*

---

3 ECLI:EU:C:2013:670.
4 ECLI:EU:C:2014:238.
5 ECLI:EU:C:2015:650.
6 ECLI:EU:C:2020:559.
7 ECLI:EU:C:2018:551.
8 ECLI:EU:C:2019:122.
9 ECLI:EU:C:2011:279.

may lawfully be imposed on the right to the protection of personal data cor-respond to those tolerated in relation to Article 8 of the Convention'.[10]

The ECtHR has, in a number of cases, similarly found a connection between personal data and the right to private life, finding that the storing of personal data falls within the ambit of Article 8 of the Convention.[11] A broad range of data has been considered by the ECtHR in the context of private life, including: telecommunications data,[12] personal information in public files,[13] analysis of internet and telephone usage,[14] DNA and fingerprint records,[15] personal information placed in an online advertisement,[16] and a record of a spent conviction.[17]

However, it is unclear how privacy as defined by the Convention will influence the interpretation of the fundamental rights and freedoms referred to in the GDPR. The GDPR has expanded the approach to data protection so that all rights and freedoms that are affected by data processing are now relevant. It incorporates all fundamental rights and freedoms recognised in the Charter:

> *'This Regulation respects all fundamental rights and observes the freedoms and principles recognised in the Charter as enshrined in the Treaties, in particular the respect for private and family life, home and communications, the protection of personal data, freedom of*

---

10 *Volker und Markus Schecke GbR*, ibid., paragraph 52.

11 *Leander v Sweden, 26 March 1987, Series A no. 116; Amann v Switzerland, Application No. 27798/95, 16 February 2000; Rotaru v Romania, Application No. 28341/95, 4 May 2000; Segerstedt- Wiberg and Others v. Sweden, no. 62332/00, 6 June 2006.*

12 Liberty & Others v United Kingdom, Application No. 58234/00, 1 July 2008.

13 *Volker und Markus Schecke GbR*, ibid.

14 *Copland v. United Kingdom, Application No. 62617/00, 3 April 2007.*

15 *S&Marper v UK, Application Nos. 30562/04 and 30566/04, 4 December 2008.*

16 *K.U. v. Finland, Application No. 2872/02, 2 December 2.*

17 *MM v U.K. Application No. 24029/07 (13 November 2012).*

thought, conscience and religion, freedom of expression and information, freedom to conduct a business, the right to an effective remedy and to a fair trial, and cultural, religious and linguistic diversity'.[18]

These fundamental rights and freedoms go beyond that of privacy and data protection, such that it must therefore be borne in mind that the GDPR can be applied by individuals to safeguard a variety of interests, albeit that the starting point will need to be some sort of interference with their personal data. Accordingly, it will be important to be aware of the jurisprudence in relation to other rights, which have been affected by the processing of personal data, and that has caused undesirable outcomes or differential treatment. This may also include the impact on a fundamental right as a result of a data subject enforcing a data protection right. In *Volker und Markus Scheke GbR*, the court described the right to data protection under the Charter as one which is not absolute, and which must be considered in relation to its function in society.[19]

Examples:

- Discrimination – *Huber v Germany, Case C-524/06, 16 December 2008.*[20]

- The right to an effective remedy – *Data Protection Commissioner v Facebook Ireland Limited, Maximillian Schrems Case C-311/18, 16 July 2020.*[21]

---

18 Recital 4 of the GDPR. 'Fundamental rights and freedoms' are referred to throughout the GDPR, see recitals 2, 10, 16, 47, 51, 69, and 113.
19 *Volker und Markus Schecke GbR*, ibid., paragraph 48.
20 ECLI:EU:C:2008:724.
21 Ibid., footnote 6.

- Freedom of expression – *Bodil Lindqvist v Åklagarkammaren i Jönköping, Case C-101/01, 6 November 2003.*[22]

- Protection of property – *Promusicae v Telefónica de España SAU, Case C-275/06, 29 January 2008,*[23]*Scarlet Extended SA v Société belge des auteurs, compositeurs et éditeurs SCRL (SABAM), Case C-70/10, 24 November 2011.*[24]

- Access to documents – *Egan & Hackett v European Parliament, Case T-190/10, 28 March 2012.*[25]

---

22 ECLI:EU:C:2003:596.
23 ECLI:EU:C:2008:54.
24 ECLI:EU:C:2011:771.
25 ECLI:EU:T:2012:165.

CHAPTER III
THE GENERAL DATA PROTECTION REGULATION AND THE DATA PROTECTION ACT 2018

The GDPR came into effect on 25 May 2018, replacing the Data Protection Directive. As it is a regulation, it has direct effect, so that it does not need to be implemented by national legislation. In the UK, the Data Protection Act 2018 ('DPA 2018') reflects the provisions of the GDPR and replaces the Data Protection Act 1998 ('DPA 1998').[1] This means that the DPA 2018 needs to be read alongside the GDPR; the position after Brexit is discussed in Chapter IX.

One of the 'new' concepts in the GDPR is the right to be forgotten, which is found in Article 17. The Data Protection Directive permitted data subjects to object to the processing of their personal data on compelling legitimate grounds relating to his or her particular situation, but did not specify erasure.[2] Under the DPA 1998, whilst it was possible to seek erasure of personal data, a data subject was only able to do so by applying to the court.

The structure of the DPA 2018 is unlike the GDPR. It replicates most of the GDPR but applies certain adaptations, restrictions and exemptions. The DPA 2018 has seven parts and data processing is separated into sectors. Parts 3 and 4 of the DPA 2018 cover law enforcement and intelligences services respectively. Part 2 of the DPA 2018 deals with 'general processing', that is, all other sectors, subject to the modifications outlined in Chapter 3 of Part 2 of the DPA 2018.

---

1   The DPA 1998 implemented the Data Protection Directive (95/46/EC).
2   See Article 14.

Before examining the right to erasure under the GDPR and the DPA 2018, I shall outline some important data protection concepts. It is necessary to understand these concepts as they are relevant to some of the practical issues that arise in seeking the right to be forgotten (discussed in Chapter VI).

Fundamental Concepts

Who has the 'right to be forgotten'?

The **data subject**[3] is defined as an identified, or identifiable natural person and has a number of rights in relation to the processing of their personal data. A data subject must be a 'natural person', which means that corporations or companies are unable to enforce the right. Although there could arguably be an exception for sole traders, or individuals whose persona cannot be separated from the organisation.[4]

The personal data may not alone identify the person but does so when combined with other information (see below *'what can be deleted?'*). There may be more than one data subject associated with the personal data.[5] For example, a postal address may reveal the identity of more than one person who lives in the household.

How is the personal data being used?

'Processing' is defined in Article 4(2) of the GDPR and Part 1 section 3(4) DPA 2018 and means anything done to data including collecting, recording, organising, storing, adapting and deleting. The processing must be wholly or partly automated. If it is not automated, it does not

---

3   GDPR Article 4(1) and Part 1 section 3(5) DPA 2018.
4   Volker und Markus Schecke GbR and Hartmut Eifert v Land Hessen.
5   *Peter Nowak v Data Protection Commissioner Case C-434/16,* 20 December 2017, ECLI:EU:C:2017:994.

fall within the scope of the GDPR and the DPA 2018 unless the personal data forms, or is intended to form, part of a filing system.[6] For example, if information, or data, is communicated over the telephone, but is not recorded, it does not fall within the scope of the data protection rules.[7]

Who can the right be enforced against?

Organisations and individuals processing personal data for professional, commercial, charitable, non-profit or public sector reasons, will come under the remit of the GDPR and are defined as either 'controllers' or 'processors'. A controller is defined in GDPR Article 4(7) and Part 2 section 6(1) DPA 2018 (for general processing) as a *person or body which, alone or jointly with others, determines the purposes and means of the processing of personal data*. Who is the controller is a question of fact. There may be situations where two organisations process the personal data and become 'joint controllers'.[8]

A processor is defined in GDPR Article 4(8) and section 5(1) DPA 2018 (general processing) as a *natural or legal person, public authority, agency or other body which processes personal data on behalf of the controller*. Processors may also be controllers in respect to certain actions taken on the same set of personal data or different sets of personal data.

Those processing personal data in a 'purely personal or household activity' will generally not be subject to the GDPR.[9] The GDPR also does not apply to processing related to activities which fall outside the scope of EU law, such as national security or foreign and security policy.[10]

---

6 Article 2(1) GDPR and Part 2, Chapter 1, section 4(2) DPA 2018.
7 See *Scott v LGBT Foundation Ltd [2020] EWHC 483 (QB)*.
8 GDPR Article 26 and Part 1, section 5(1) DPA 2018.
9 GDPR Article 2(c). See also Chapter VI of this book, under practical issues for data subjects.
10 See GDPR Article 2(2)(a) and recital 16.

Where does it apply?

According to Article 3 of the GDPR, it applies in the following situations:

(1) When a controller or processor is 'established' in the EU (regardless of whether or not the processing takes place in the EU);[11]

(2) Where there is 'monitoring' of EU data subjects, or the offering of goods or services to EU data subjects, even if the controller or processor in not in the EU;

(3) Where the controller or processor are not in the EU, but Member State law applies by virtue of public international law.

Knowing when the GDPR applies is not always a straightforward analysis. It is important to understand that its applicability is not confined to the nationality of the data subjects, the location where the data controllers are legally or officially incorporated, or where the processing takes place. This territorial scope is identical in the DPA 2018.

What obligations do controllers and processors have?

When processing personal data, controllers and processors must adhere to the six principles in Article 5 of the GDPR:[12]

(1) Lawfulness, fairness and transparency;

(2) Purpose limitation;

(3) Data minimisation;

---

11 This was one of the questions put to the CJEU in the *Google Spain* case, see Chapter IV of this book.

12 Part 1 section 2 and Part 2 section 4 of DPA 2018.

(4) Accuracy;

(5) Storage Limitation;

(6) Integrity and confidentiality.

To comply with the principles, there are a number of obligations that are set out in Chapters II, III, IV and V of the GDPR.

What can be deleted?

Under the GDPR, data subjects have rights over their personal data. Personal data is given a broad definition in the GDPR. It is defined in Article 4(1):

> *'Personal data' means any information relating to an identified or identifiable natural person 'data subject'; an identifiable person is one who can be identified, directly or indirectly, in particular by reference to an identifier such as a name, an identification number, location data, an online identifier or to one or more factors specific to the physical, physiological, genetic, mental, economic, cultural or social identity of that natural person'.*

'Any information' means that any format or type of information – video, written records, audio files, photographs etc. – is subject to the GDPR. The information does not need to relate to an individual in their private or family life, the approach is 'agnostic' in this regard.

The information 'relates' to a person where there is a relationship that can be established between the data and a person because of its content, the purpose for which it is being used, or the consequences of its use on a person.[13]

---

13 See Article 29 Working Party 'Opinion 4/2007 on the concept of personal data', 20 June 2007.

Where a controller processes personal data that on its own does not identify a person (referred to as 'pseudonymised' data) but that when combined with other information it becomes possible to identify a person, then the pseudonymised data falls within the GDPR rules. It does not matter if the 'other information' is held by a different controller, organisation, or is available elsewhere.[14] Recital 26 gives some assistance in the question of whether or not a person is 'identifiable' from the pseudonymised data stating: *"account should be taken of all the means reasonably likely to be used, such as singling out, either by the controller or by another person to identify the natural person directly or indirectly"*.

Data that that has been anonymised is no longer considered to be personal data under the GDPR. There is often confusion between pseudonymised (or de-identified data) and anonymised data. Often controllers refer to personal data being anonymised when in fact they have been pseudonymised.[15]

Recital 30 of the GDPR explains that online identifiers are those identifiers provided by *'devices, applications, tools and protocols'*, from which a person may be identified by combining those identifiers with unique identifiers and information received by servers. These identifiers, combined with other information, may be used to create profiles of persons, and identify them.

The special categories

There are also what are known as 'special categories' of personal data, over which controllers have additional responsibilities given their sensitive nature. The special categories are listed in GDPR Article 9(1) and are personal data relating to:

---

14 See *Patrick Breyer v Bundesrepublik Deutschland CJEU Case C-582/14*, 19 October 2016, ECLI: EU:C:2016:779.

15 For the definition in the GDPR, see Article 4(5).

- Racial or ethnic origin

- Political opinion

- Religious or philosophical beliefs

- Trade union membership

- Health

- Sex life or sexual orientation

- Genetic data

- Biometric data (processed to uniquely identify a person)

Processing by a controller of these categories of personal data is prohibited, unless one of the lawful processing conditions under GDPR Article 9(2) or Schedule 1 to the DPA 2018 applies. Controllers must still comply with all other GDPR principles, including having a lawful basis in Article 6(1).[16]

The Right to be Forgotten in the GDPR and DPA 2018

The right to be forgotten is found in Article 17 of the GDPR. According to Article 17(1):

> *'The data subject shall have the right to obtain from the controller the erasure of personal data concerning him or her without undue delay and the controller shall have the obligation to erase personal data without undue delay'.*

There are six grounds where the right to erasure applies. However, if it is necessary for the controller to process the personal data for one of the 'listed purposes' (essentially, exemptions) in Article 17(3), then the con-

---

16 Part 2 sections 10(1) to (3) DPA 2018.

troller will not be obliged to comply with the request. There is no need for the data subject to prove harm, or provide a reason for the erasure request, so long as one of the grounds below is satisfied.

The Grounds

The grounds are as follows:

Ground	Reference	Description
1	Article 17(1)(a)	The personal data are no longer necessary in relation to the purposes for which they were collected or otherwise processed.
2	Article 17(1)(b)	The data subject withdraws consent on which the processing is based according to point (a) of Article 6(1), or point (a) of Article 9(2), and where there is no other legal ground for the processing.
3	Article 17(1)(c)	The data subject objects to the processing pursuant to Article 21(1) and there are no overriding legitimate grounds for the processing, or the data subject objects to the processing pursuant to Article 21(2).
4	Article 17(1)(d)	The personal data have been unlawfully processed.
5	Article 17(1)(e)	The personal data have to be erased for compliance with a legal obligation in Union or Member State law to which the controller is subject.
6	Article 17(1)(f)	The personal data have been collected in relation to the offer of information society services referred to in Article 8(1).

Ground 1: The personal data are no longer necessary in relation to the purposes for which the data were collected or otherwise processed

Purpose limitation is the principle that controllers only collect personal data for a specific and legitimate purpose, and do not further process the personal data in a manner that is incompatible with the original purpose.[17] The principles of purpose limitation and data minimisation mean that where personal data is no longer required for the purposes for which it was collected, it should be deleted. Controllers are obliged to provide data subjects with information about the processing of their personal data (see GDPR Articles 13 and 14), including how long the personal data will be stored. This information is most commonly made available in a 'privacy notice'. Ideally controllers should have established procedures to track the personal data that is processed, and to ensure that these principles are adhered to.

There may be different processing operations performed on personal data for multiple purposes, all of which should have been specified in the privacy notice to the data subject. For example, a consumer may give an online retailer their name and home address to purchase a product. The online retailer is likely to use this personal data for more than one purpose: to send the consumer the product, and also to process the payment for the product.

Ground 1 does not apply where it is still necessary for the controller to process the data for the specific purpose upon which it relies. The onus is on the controller to show that it is still necessary for it to process the data so that it cannot comply with the erasure request. It may be that the controller can delete the personal data in relation to one purpose, but not for another.

---

17 Article 5(1)(b) GDPR.

It has been established that 'necessary' is interpreted in data protection as 'reasonably' necessary rather than 'strictly' necessary.[18] If the processing of the personal data is not reasonably necessary for the purpose specified, the controller must comply with the request for erasure.

From the wording of Article 17(1)(a), it appears the reference point for determining the purpose is at the time of collection from the data subject. This is particularly relevant where the controller has received the personal data from another controller. The point at which the purpose is determined for the evaluation of the request is not when the second controller <u>received</u> the data, but when the first controller <u>collected</u> the data.

GDPR recital 50 is relevant for the legitimacy of further processing of personal data:

> *'the processing of personal data for purposes other than those for which the personal data were initially collected should be allowed only where the processing is compatible with the purposes for which personal data were initially collected.'*

Where a controller further processes personal data for a purpose that is compatible with the initial purpose, no separate legal basis is required. To assess whether or not the purpose for the further processing is compatible (and lawful), recital 50 outlines some factors to consider:

➢ Any link between the initial purpose(s) and the purpose(s) of the further processing;

➢ The context in which the personal data was collected;

---

18 *South Lanarkshire Council v Scottish IC [2013] UKSC 55*, paragraph 27.

> ➤ The reasonable expectations of the data subject on further use of their personal data, based on the relationship with the controller;

> ➤ The consequences of the further processing on the data subject;

> ➤ The existence (or not) of appropriate safeguards.

Ground 2: The data subject withdraws consent

The GDPR has a stricter definition of consent than under the Data Protection Directive. Under the GDPR consent must be *informed* consent, such that inactivity or silence will not be valid. For consent to be valid, it must be:[19]

- Clearly distinguished

- Intelligible

- Easily accessible

- Freely given

- Specific

There are further caveats:

- The data subject must have the ability to withdraw consent as easily as he or she gives consent.

- Consent cannot be 'bundled' together for different purposes.

---

19 GDPR Article 7 and Article 6(1)(a); see also recitals 42 and 43.

If any one of the above elements or further caveats is not met, then the controller does not have valid consent to process the data.[20] Where the controller is processing the personal data on the basis of consent for multiple purposes, it will need consent for all of those purposes.[21] The underlying principle is that a data subject gives consent to process his or her personal data, on the understanding that they are in control of that data, and that it will be processed only for the specified purpose for which it has been given.

Where consent applies to the processing of one of the special categories of data, according to GDPR Article 9(2)(a), it must be explicit.[22] This means that the data subject must give an express statement of consent.[23] The GDPR does not prescribe how a controller should obtain explicit consent, but the EDPB suggests that where appropriate a controller should ideally receive a written statement signed by the data subject, or some other recorded confirmation.[24]

Further processing of the personal data (for the same or a different purposes) should not be based on another lawful ground other than consent, once that consent is withdrawn. That is, generally, the controller should not switch its legal basis. If consent is withdrawn, all data processing operations based on consent must stop, and the personal data be deleted unless there is another lawful basis for continuing to hold or

---

20 See the recent investigation by CNIL into Google's reliance on consent to process personal data for advert personalisation. Google was fined 50 million euros for lack of transparency, inadequate information and lack of valid consent. The EDPB press release is available here: https://edpb.europa.eu/news/national-news/2019/cnils-restricted-committee-imposes-financial-penalty-50-million-euros_en

21 See GDPR recital 32.

22 GDPR Article 9(2) outlines other exceptions, but for the majority of controllers explicit consent will be required.

23 European Data Protection Board 'Guidelines 05/2020 on consent under Regulation 2016/679', adopted 4 May 2020, paragraph 93.

24 Ibid.

process the personal data. This means that where a controller needs to process personal data for multiple purposes, it must carefully assess the legal bases on which it intends to rely, before collecting the data.

The lawful grounds and purpose for each processing operation must be determined at the outset.[25] If the controller wants to continue to process personal data on another lawful basis, it cannot 'silently migrate from consent' to another lawful basis without first informing the data subject.[26] The controller is obliged to assess whether or not it is appropriate to continue to process personal data once consent has been withdrawn.[27]

The timing of the withdrawal of the consent is not defined in Article 17(1)(b); it is not clear if the action of withdrawing consent must occur before the erasure request is made. For the avoidance of doubt, the data subject should make clear when making an erasure request – if consent has not been previously withdrawn – that the request also constitutes notice of withdrawal of consent.

Ground 3: The data subject objects to the processing

For this ground, it is necessary to examine the right to object to processing provided by Article 21 of the GDPR. Article 21 sets out a number of circumstances under which data subjects have a right to object to a controller processing their personal data. There are five situations outlined in Article 21 when a data subject can object:

i. The personal data is processed under GDPR Article 6(1)(e) where '*processing is necessary for the performance of a task carried*

---

25 Ibid., paragraphs 116 to 120.
26 Ibid., paragraph 120.
27 Ibid., paragraph 118.

out in the public interest or in the exercise of official authority vested in the controller';

ii. The personal data is processed under GDPR Article 6(1)(f) where *'processing is necessary for the purposes of the legitimate interests pursued by the controller or by a third party, except where such interests are overridden by the interests or fundamental rights and freedoms of the data subject which require protection of personal data, in particular where the data subject is a child'.*

iii. Where the personal data is processed for direct marketing purposes;[28]

iv. *In the context of the use of information society services, and notwithstanding Directive 2002/58/EC, the data subject may exercise his or her right to object by automated means using technical specifications;*[29]

v. Where personal data are being processed for scientific, historical research or statistical purposes under GDPR Article 89(1).

According to Article 21(1), in reference to the first two grounds listed above (i) and (ii), the controller is required to assess the 'particular situation' of the data subject. There are two possible scenarios where the controller is not obliged to comply with the request:

1. where it can demonstrate compelling legitimate grounds which override the interests, rights and freedoms of the data subject; or

---

28 See GDPR Article 21(3).

29 See GDPR Article 21(4); Directive 2002/58/EC of the European Parliament and of the Council of 12 July 2002 concerning the processing of personal data and the protection of privacy in the electronic communications sector ('ePrivacy Directive').

2. for the establishment, exercise or defence of legal claims.

The right to object to processing for the purposes of direct marketing (in (iii) above) is an absolute right and there are no exemptions that the controller can invoke. Whilst there is as yet no case law on the point, it seems logical that if an erasure request is made in relation to the objection of the use of the personal data for direct marketing, then once the ground is made out (i.e. Article 17(1)(c) and 21(2)), there is no recourse to the use of the exemptions in Article 17(3), given the absolute nature of Article 21(2) and the wording of 17(1)(c).

Article 21(2) also applies to the processing of personal data for profiling related to direct marketing. This could extend to situations where a controller is creating a profile with the intention of its use for direct marketing, even if it has not yet done so.

GDPR Article 89(1) – where personal data are being processed for scientific, historical research or statistical purposes – is discussed below under 'exemption 4'.

The timing of the objection is not specified in the GDPR in reference to Article 17. It is advisable that a data subject making an erasure request on this ground, should make clear that the request also constitutes notice that the data subject objects to the processing of the personal data.

Ground 4: The personal data is being unlawfully processed

There are six lawful bases for processing personal data, set out in GDPR Article 6. Personal data will be 'unlawfully' processed where any of the requirements to satisfy the grounds in Article 6 are not met. The lawful bases are:

(a) Consent (where consent is held to the GDPR standard);

(b) Contract (where the processing must be necessary for the contract, or as part of pre-contractual steps);

(c) The legitimate interests of the controller;

(d) Vital interests of the data subject or another natural person;

(e) Public task;

(f) Legal obligation.

Consent has been explained above under 'ground 2'.

A controller may process the personal data to give effect to a **contract** with the data subject. This basis can also be used for data processing that is undertaken at the request of the data subject prior to entering into a contract. The contract must be between the controller and the data subject. Processing to give effect to contractual obligations with a third party are not covered by this basis.

Further, the data processing must be <u>necessary</u> to provide the contract or service. This is an objective fact-based assessment and is not determined by what the parties have agreed in the contract. If the processing is necessary, not for the contract, but for the controller's business purposes, then the legal basis of legitimate interest is more appropriate.

The legal basis of **legitimate interest** involves a balancing exercise between the 'interests or fundamental rights and freedoms of the data subject' and the legitimate interests pursued by the controller.[30] Recital 75 explains that 'the risk to the rights and freedoms of natural persons' will vary in likelihood and severity depending upon the context of the data processing operation. The potential negative outcomes include physical, material, or non-material damage (see Chapter VIII); examples

---

30 GDPR Article 6(1)(f).

given include discrimination, identity theft, fraud and damage to reputation.[31]

The legitimate interest must be: linked to the data processing operation, necessary to the processing operation and not speculative.[32] If there is another more suitable lawful basis, or less intrusive processing is possible, then the use of legitimate interest as a basis will not be valid and the controller should consider whether another lawful ground in Article 6(1) is more suitable. The GDPR, in recitals 47 to 49, gives examples of legitimate interest as: fraud prevention, direct marketing, intra-company data transfers and network security. Other common areas are also commercial interests and research.

It may be necessary to process personal data where the '**vital interest**' interest of the data subject is at stake. This legal basis for processing is generally uncontroversial: it is applicable when it is necessary in order to save a person's life. GDPR recital 46 describes the basis as suitable where '*it is necessary to protect an interest which is essential for the life of the data subject or that of another natural person*'.

Note that where the processing is based on the vital interest of a different person to the data subject, that the controller must be satisfied that another legal basis is not suitable. There is some overlap between vital interest and the public interest, for example where processing occurs for humanitarian emergencies.[33] Vital interest will most often involve the processing of health data, which is a special category of data, and means that the controller will also need to comply with GDPR Article 9(2).

For processing to be necessary for the performance of a task carried out in the '**public interest**' or '**exercise of official authority**', there must be a

---

31 See GDPR recital 75.
32 Article 29 Working Party 'Opinion 06/2014 on the Notion of Legitimate Interests of the Data Controller under Article 7 of Directive 95/46/EC', adopted on 9 April 2014.
33 See GDPR recital 46.

specific task that is being carried out, or the exercise of a duty, that is laid down by law. However, there need not be explicit statutory provision for this basis to be valid. According to recital 41 of the GDPR, so long as there is a legal basis or legislative measure that is clear and precise in application, and foreseeable to data subjects, then it will be possible to rely on it.

Part 1, Section 8 of the DPA 2018 describes this basis as appropriate where the processing is necessary for:

➢ The administration of Justice;

➢ The exercise of a function of either House of Parliament;

➢ The exercise of a function conferred on a person by an enactment or rule of law;

➢ The exercise of a function of the Crown, a Minister of the Crown or a government department, or

➢ An activity that supports or promotes democratic engagement.

See also, DPA 2018 Schedule 1 paragraphs 6 and 7.

Legal obligation

The final legal basis is where the controller has a **legal obligation** to process the personal data. This applies where there is a legal obligation that is laid down by law – either by statute, or in order to comply with the common law. The controller must be able to point to the specific legal obligation. For example, it will most likely be obliged to keep certain records in order to comply with a request from tax authorities. Note however that a contractual obligation with a third party does not constitute a legal obligation for the purposes of this legal basis.

The data protection principles

It is also arguable that where personal data is being processed on a valid legal basis, but without complying with other data protection principles in GDPR Article 5 (see above), that the personal data is being processed 'unlawfully' for the purposes of ground 4.

Ground 5: The personal data must be deleted to comply with a legal obligation

It may be necessary for controllers to delete information to comply with a legal obligation. For example, Article 6(1) of the Privacy and Electronic Communications Directive 2002/58/EC on Privacy and Electronic Communications ('ePrivacy Directive') requires a provider of a public communications network, or publicly available electronic communications service, to erase (or anonymise) its users traffic data.

Ground 5 could be particularly relevant at the present time given the concerns about the collection of personal data to tackle the Covid-19 pandemic and the long term use of that data.[34] The EDPB has recommended that personal data collected for contact tracing, in particular through mobile phone applications ('apps'), should only be kept for the duration of the crisis, and thereafter either erased or anonymised.[35] The European Commission has recommended that so-called 'sunset clauses'[36] are introduced so that processing does not go beyond what is strictly necessary.[37] The UK parliamentary Joint Committee on Human Rights has proposed a Bill to regulate the use of information for contact

---

34 See: Joint Committee on Human Rights, 'Human Rights and The Government's Response to Covid-19: Digital Contact Tracing', 6 May 2020.

35 European Data Protection Board 'Guidelines 04/2020 on the use of location data and contact tracing tools in the context of the Covid-19 outbreak, adopted on 21 April 2020', paragraph 35.

36 Stock, M., Orrell T. (2020), "COVID-19 Data and Data Sharing Agreements: the Potential of Sunset Clauses and Sunset Provisions", SDSN-TreNDS.

tracing and connected purposes, including the deletion of the data once it is no longer required.[38]

It is not clear how ground 5 would apply to a third party who has received the data from a controller who is subject to a legal obligation to delete the data, but to which the third party is not subject.

Ground 6: The personal data was collected in relation to the offer of information society services to a child

Children are recognised in the GDPR as affording special protection. According to GDPR Article 6: '*fundamental rights and freedoms of the data subject which require protection of personal data, in particular where the data subject is a child*'. Recital 38 highlights that '*children merit specific protection with regard to their personal data, as they may be less aware of the risks, consequences and safeguards concerned and their rights in relation to the processing of personal data*'.

Recital 65 states that the right to be forgotten is '*relevant in particular where the data subject has given his or her consent as a child and is not fully aware of the risks involved by the processing, and later wants to remove such personal data, especially on the internet*'.

The fact that the consent was given by someone with parental responsibility, does not prevent the data subject from requesting erasure on the basis of Article 17(1)(f); that is, the withdrawal of consent does not have

---

37 European Commission Recommendation (EU) 2020/518 of 8 April 2020 'on a common Union toolbox for the use of technology and data to combat and exit from the COVID-19 crisis, in particular concerning mobile applications and the use of anonymised mobility data'.

38 UK parliamentary Joint Committee on Human Rights proposed Bill, accessible here:
https://publications.parliament.uk/pa/jt5801/jtselect/jtrights/correspondence/Letter-to-Rt-Hon-Matt-Hancock-MP-Secretary-of-State-for-HSC-Draft-Bill.pdf

to be parental consent. It also applies where the data subject is no longer a child.

An 'information society service' is defined in Article 1(1)(b) of Directive (EU) 2015/1535 as:[39]

> 'Any service normally provided for remuneration, at a distance, by electronic means and at the individual request of a recipient of services'.
>
> For the purposes of this definition:
>
> (i) 'at a distance' means that the service is provided without the parties being simultaneously present;
>
> (ii) 'by electronic means' means that the service is sent initially and received at its destination by means of electronic equipment for the processing (including digital compression) and storage of data, and entirely transmitted, conveyed and received by wire, by radio, by optical means or by other electromagnetic means;
>
> (iii) 'at the individual request of a recipient of services' means that the service is provided through the transmission of data on individual request.'

The definition captures the majority of online services, such as websites, applications, search engines, online content and video services.[40] 'Remuneration' is interpreted broadly, so that the definition also includes those services that rely on advertising revenue rather than payment from

---

39 'Of the European Parliament and the Council of 9 September 2015 laying down a procedure for the provision of information in the field of technical regulations and of rules on Information Society services'.

40 In Annex I to the Directive, there is an indicative list of services that are not covered by the definition.

the user directly.[41] Part 1, section 9 DPA 2018 excludes preventative or counselling services from the definition.

Article 8(1) of the GDPR sets out the conditions that apply for a child to validly consent to information society services. Each Member State may decide the age limit that applies to define the data subject as a child. In the UK, the age limit is 13.[42] Note that the Information Commissioner's Office ('ICO') also considers an information society service as offered 'directly to a child' where the service is made available to any user without an age restriction.[43]

A controller falling within the definition of an information society service should therefore be aware that even if the service they offer is not made to a child, that they may still receive a right to be forgotten request under this ground. Controllers should also be aware of the ICO Age Appropriate Design Code, which came into force on 2 September 2020.

---

41 Case 352/85, Bond van Adverteerders v the Netherlands [1988] ECR 2085.
42 Part 1, section 9 DPA 2018.
43 See the ICO Guidance 'Children and the GDPR'.

The Exemptions

The exemptions are as follows:

Exemption	Reference	Description
1	Article 17(3)(a)	For exercising the right of freedom of expression and information.
2	Article 17(3)(b)	For compliance with a legal obligation which requires processing by Union or Member State law to which the controller is subject or for the performance of a task carried out in the public interest or in the exercise of official authority vested in the controller.
3	Article 17(3)(c)	For reasons of public interest in the area of public health in accordance with points (h) and (i) of Article 9(2) as well as Article 9(3).
4	Article 17(3)(d)	For archiving purposes in the public interest, scientific or historical research purposes or statistical purposes in accordance with Article 89(1) in so far as the right referred to in paragraph 1 is likely to render impossible or seriously impair the achievement of the objective of that processing.
5	Article 17(3)(e)	For the establishment, exercise or defence of legal claims.

If the processing of the personal data is 'necessary' for one of the exemptions listed above, then the controller need not erase the data. It is not for the data subject to establish that an exemption does not apply. The approach is first to establish whether one of the conditions in Article 17(1) is met, only then can the controller review its obligations and see if an exemption applies. To comply with the data protection principles of transparency and fairness, the controller should inform the data subject of the exemption it relies upon and give reasons as to why the exemption applies.

Note that the exemption applies 'to the extent that processing is necessary'. If there are other alternative methods of processing, then the controller should rely on one of the exemptions with the application of modifications. For example it may be possible to redact the personal data or apply other technical measures that either pseudonymise or anonymise the data.

The exemptions are interpreted strictly and narrowly, given that the effect of them is to override the fundamental rights of the data subject. It will be necessary to reflect upon Articles 7 and 8 of the Charter and potentially also certain Convention rights when determining whether or not an exemption applies.

Exemption 1: The right of freedom of expression

The right to be forgotten has been particularly controversial in the context of the right to freedom of expression and information. There is no specific guidance within the GDPR on this exemption. Article 85 directs EU Member States to make their own provisions in law that reconcile personal data protection with 'the right of freedom of expression and information', including processing for journalistic purposes and the purposes of academic, artistic or literary expression. Recital 153 also highlights the inclusion of the particular processing activities of news archives and press libraries.

Given the precise wording of Article 17(3), an assessment of the link between the processing and its necessity in the exercise of the right to freedom of expression and information will be required. It may be that the processing of the data, when it was collected, was necessary to exercise the right to freedom of expression, but that at the point in time the application for erasure is made, that this link no longer exists. It cannot be assumed that the exemption will automatically apply to media or journalism outlets, or that it won't apply to artistic or literary organisations, depending on the context of the processing.

The recent UK case of *NT1 & NT2 v Google LLC [2018] EWHC 799 (QB)* in the High Court considered delisting requests and the right to freedom of expression and information, this case and two other cases in the CJEU that also analysed the exemption are reviewed in Chapter VII. There is substantial case law related to Article 11 of the Charter, and Article 10 of the Convention, the application of which will depend on the specific facts and context of the erasure request.

Exemption 2: Compliance with a legal obligation or public interest

Article 17(3)(b) is in essence the lawful grounds of Article 6(1)(c) 'legal obligation' and 6(1)(e) 'public interest or in the exercise of official authority'. See 'ground 4' above.

Exemption 3: For reasons of public interest in the area of health

The reference to Article 9 in Article 17(3)(c) implies that this exemption only applies to personal data that is in the special categories and not 'regular' personal data.[44] On this view, the result is that 'ordinary' personal data does not fall within this exemption such that if it is processed for reasons of public health in the public interest it should be de-

---

44 Some practitioners take a different view. See Jay, Malcolm, Parry, Townsend and Bapat, *Guide to the General Data Protection Regulation, A Companion to Data Protection Law and Practice,* (2017), p.276.

leted if requested. This point has not yet been raised and could be a future area of contention.

Recital 54 highlights that processing for reasons of public interest in the areas of public health should be subject to measures designed to protect individual's rights and fundamental freedoms. 'Public health' is interpreted as defined in Regulation (EC) No 1338/2008.[45] It will be difficult to show that the exemption applies where the processing is not based on a specific law for the public interest in purposes of public health.

Recital 54 also explicitly states that the processing of data in this context should '*not result in personal data being processed for other purposes by third parties such as employers or insurance and banking companies*'. This has become a particularly topical area in data protection since the Covid-19 pandemic, which has brought into sharp focus the collection of health data and the public-private partnerships that have evolved as a result.[46]

Exemption 4: For archiving in the public interest, scientific, historical or statistical purposes

GDPR Article 89(1) explains that processing for these purposes should include appropriate safeguards to protect the rights and freedoms of the data subject and controllers should apply technical and organisational measures, in particular, to ensure data minimisation is achieved. According to recital 159, the processing of personal data for scientific research purposes should be '*interpreted in a broad manner including for*

---

45 'Of the European Parliament and of the Council of 16 December 2008 on Community statistics on public health and health and safety at work (Text with EEA relevance)'. See also GDPR recital 54.

46 See 'UK government releases NHS Covid19 data deals with big tech', 5 June 2020, available: https://www.foxglove.org.uk/news/breakthrough-uk-government-releases-nhs-covid19-data-deals-with-big-tech

example technological development and demonstration, fundamental research, applied research and privately funded research'. Recital 162 highlights the need to ensure statistical confidentiality and that the result of the statistical processing is not personal data, but aggregate data. The result of which should not be used for measures or decisions that impact a particular individual.

The wording in Article 17(3)(d) is that the exemption applies *'in so far as the right referred to in paragraph 1 is likely to render impossible or seriously impair the achievement of the objectives of that processing'*. This means that if it is possible to erase the data without it preventing the objective(s) of the processing, then the controller cannot rely on the exemption and must erase the data.

Exemption 5: For the establishment, exercise or defence of legal claims

There is little guidance on this exemption, although it is a basis that appears in other areas of the GDPR.[47] According to recital 52 it may involve court proceedings, or an 'administrative or out-of-court procedure'. In the DPA 1998, Schedule 3, paragraph 6, the equivalent provision that permitted an exemption for the purpose of dealing with legal claims, expressly included prospective legal proceedings. This is mirrored in parts of the DPA 2018, in the schedules that govern the exemptions and conditions (explained further below in 'DPA 2018').[48]

---

47 See GDPR Articles 18(1)(c) and 21(1) and recital 65.

48 For example in the DPA 2018 in Schedule 1, Part 3, paragraph 33 (in relation to criminal convictions) and Schedule 2, paragraph 5(3) (in relation to information required to be disclosed in connection with legal proceedings in the context of GDPR Article 23(1).

Informing other Controllers

GDPR Article 17(2) obliges a controller that has *'made the personal data public'* and has received a valid erasure request to inform other controllers who are processing the personal data. Recital 66 explains how the right to be forgotten has been intentionally strengthened so that the controller must inform other controllers to *'erase any links to, or copies or replications of those personal data'* that are the subject of the request.

The extent of the responsibility of controllers to inform other controllers about the erasure request will depend on the circumstances. Controllers are expected to take *'reasonable steps, taking into account available technology and the means available to the controller, including technical measures, to inform the controllers which are processing the personal data of the data subjects' request'.*[49]

There is also an obligation in GDPR Article 19 for the controller to communicate the request to *'each recipient to whom the personal data have been disclosed, unless this proves impossible or involves disproportionate effort. The controller shall inform the data subject about those recipients if the data subject requests it'.* The difference between Article 17(2) and 19 is that in the former, where the controller has made the information public, it applies to <u>any</u> controller, whereas the latter concerns direct recipients of the data from the data controller. The scope of 'made public' is not clarified in the GDPR or the DPA 2018.

The DPA 2018 Exemptions

The DPA 2018 structure has been outlined in the introduction to this chapter; it incorporates the various derogations, restrictions and adaptations provided for in the GDPR. There are also purpose-based exemptions, which cover areas which are outside the scope of EU law (na-

---

49 GDPR Article 17(2).

tional security, defence, law enforcement). The exemptions that apply to certain data types are found in the schedules. For example confidential references, exam papers, negotiations, health data, social work data, education data, child abuse data are exempt from some aspects of the GDPR.

Those that are exempt from GDPR Article 17 are found in:

> ➢ Schedule 2, paragraph 2 (crime)

> ➢ Schedule 2, paragraph 4(2) (immigration)

> ➢ Schedule 2, paragraph 5 (legal proceedings)

> ➢ Schedule 2, paragraph 6 (regulatory functions designed to protect the public)

> ➢ Schedule 2, paragraph 26 (freedom of expression)

> ➢ Schedule 3 paragraph 1 (health, social work, education and child abuse)

CHAPTER IV
THE RIGHT TO BE
FORGOTTEN CASE:

Google Spain SL, Google Inc. v Agencia Española de Protección de Datos (AEPD), Mario Costeja González, Court of Justice (Grand Chamber), Case C-131/12, 13 May 2014

The Facts

In March 2010, Mr Mario Costeja González made a complaint to Spain's Data Protection Agency ('AEPD') against the newspaper publisher La Vanguardia Ediciones SL, Google Spain and Google Inc. The complaint related to newspaper articles that appeared in Google Inc.'s search engine results against his name. The articles, from 1998, referred to him in relation to a real estate auction connected with attachment proceedings to recover social security debts.

Mr González wanted La Vanguardia either to remove or alter those pages so that his name no longer appeared, or to use certain tools made available by search engines in order to protect the data. He also wanted Google Inc. to remove or conceal the personal data relating to him so that they would no longer be included in the search results in the links to La Vanguardia. He argued that the attachment proceedings had been fully resolved for a number of years and that reference to them was now entirely irrelevant.

On 30 July 2010, the AEPD rejected his complaint in relation to La Vanguardia, on the basis that the publication of the information was legally justified, because it had been ordered by the Ministry of Labour and Social Affairs to give maximum publicity to the auction. However, the complaint against Google Inc. and Google Spain was upheld. The AEPD was of the view that the operators of search engines are subject to data protection legislation because they are responsible for the processing of personal data and act as intermediaries in the information society. As such, the AEPD concluded that it had the right to require them to withdraw personal data when the location and dissemination of that data compromises the fundamental right to data protection, without it being necessary to erase the data at source.

Google Inc. appealed against the decision, bringing proceedings before Spain's National High Court, which in turn referred questions to the CJEU for a preliminary ruling.

The questions referred to the court can be summarised as follows:[1]

1 How is 'establishment' in the Data Protection Directive to be interpreted when a data controller is based outside of the Member State, but has a subsidiary based in the Member State that is processing data for a purpose not directly related to the main operations of the data controller.

2 Is Google Inc. considered as processing personal data, as interpreted as by Article 2(b) of the Data Protection Directive, by providing content that consists of locating information published, or included on the internet by third parties, indexing it automatically, storing it temporarily and finally making it available to internet users?

3 If yes, must Article 2(d) of the Data Protection Directive be interpreted as meaning that the undertaking managing an internet search result is to be regarded as a 'controller' of the personal data contained in the web pages that it indexes?

---

1 I have summarised only those questions addressed by the court, others became irrelevant as a result of its conclusions with respect to those questions it did in fact address.

4 If yes to question (3), may the data protection authority directly impose a requirement on the search engine operator to withdraw an item of information published by third parties that it has indexed, without communicating in advance with the owner of the web page on which the information is located?

5 If yes to question (4), would the obligation of operators of search engines to protect those rights be excluded when the information that contains the personal data has been lawfully published by third parties and is kept on the web page from which it originates?

6 Do the rights to erasure and blocking of data provided for in Article 12(b) and Article 14 of the Data Protection Directive extend to enabling the data subject to prevent search engines indexing information relating to him personally, even if lawfully published on third parties' web pages, on the basis that such information should not be known to internet users when he considers that it may be prejudicial to him or he wishes it to be 'consigned to oblivion'?

The Judgment

i 'Establishment' (Question (1))

On the question of establishment, the CJEU referred to recital 19 in the preamble to the Data Protection Directive, which states that 'establishment on the territory of a Member State implies the effective and real exercise of activity through stable arrangements'. The court concluded that Google Spain constitutes a subsidiary of Google Inc. on Spanish territory and is therefore an 'establishment' within the meaning of Article 4(1) of the Directive.[2]

---

2 Paragraph 49 of the judgment.

Google Inc. had argued that because Google Inc. operates the search engine, and Google Spain was responsible for advertising activities in Spain, that the criterion in Article 4(1) – that it is also necessary for the processing to be 'carried out in the context of the activities' of an establishment of the controller – was not met. The CJEU disagreed, stating that the processing of personal data in Spain for the purpose of a search engine, was clearly in the context of the activities of selling advertising space offered by that search engine, because it serves to make the service it offers more profitable.[3] Those activities, it found, were *'inextricably linked'*.[4]

ii 'Processing' and 'Controller' (Questions (2) and (3))

The CJEU decided that Google Inc. must be considered to be 'processing' personal data by the fact that its search service is performing operations that is expressly referred to in Article 2(b) of the Data Protection Directive.[5] Google Inc. is *'exploring the internet automatically, constantly and systematically in search of the information which is published there'* and subsequently retrieves, records, organises by indexing, stores and then discloses by making it available in the form of a list of search results. The fact that the search engine does not alter the data made available by the third party was irrelevant to this conclusion.

On the question of whether or not Google Inc. is the controller in relation to the personal data that it processes for search results listings, the CJEU decided that it was, because it determines the purposes and means of the processing in the context of its activity of operating a search engine.[6] This activity is distinct from that of the publishers of websites, which are merely loading the information onto webpages. The court highlighted the important role that search engines occupy in the dissemination of data, which makes a search of a person's name reveal

---

3 Paragraph 55 to 56.
4 Paragraph 56.
5 Paragraph 28.
6 Paragraphs 33 to 35.

information that may otherwise not have been found.[7] Further, the manner in which a search engine collates information into a list has the result of providing a detailed profile of the data subject. As a result, *'the activity of a search engine is therefore liable to affect significantly, and additionally compared with that of the publishers of websites, the fundamental rights to privacy and to the protection of personal data'* and must ensure it meets the requirements of the Data Protection Directive so that the right to privacy may 'actually' be achieved.[8]

   iii Data supervisory authorities and the publisher (Question (4))

Given the view of the court on the application of Articles 12(b) and 14 of the Data Protection Directive, it followed that a supervisory authority or judicial authority may order the search engine operator to remove the search results list against a person's name, without either ordering or pre-supposing the removal of that information from the publisher's webpage.[9] Primarily this is because the data processing of the search engine operator in its business activities can be distinguished from the data processing of the website publisher.[10]

There may be circumstances where the data subject has a justified delisting request against the search engine operator, but not against the publisher. The latter may validly invoke a derogation under the Data Protection Directive, most likely the 'journalistic purposes' derogation, but that derogation would not apply to the search engine operator.[11] Further, the legitimate interests in processing personal data (if this legal basis of processing is relied upon by different parties) may not be the same for the different controllers such that the consequences on the private life of the data subject may also differ.[12] In this case, search en-

---

7 Paragraph 36.
8 Paragraph 38.
9 Paragraph 82.
10 Paragraph 83.
11 Paragraph 85.
12 Paragraph 86.

gine operators *'play a decisive role in the dissemination of that informa-tion'* and make access to information relating to a person *'appreciably easier for any internet user'* such that the interference with the data sub-ject's private life may be more significant than by the publisher of the information on a particular website.[13]

iv   The search engine versus the publisher (Question (5))

Google Inc. submitted two points to the CJEU. First, that a request for removal from its search engine result list must be directed to the pub-lisher of the website where the content was available, because it is the publisher who is best placed to determine the lawfulness of the publica-tion, and who has the means to either restrict or make the information inaccessible. Second, if the search engine operator were to remove the information from its indexes, it would be infringing upon the funda-mental rights of publishers of websites, other internet users and the op-erators themselves.

The CJEU referred to Articles 7 and 8 of the Charter (set out in Chapter II) and the fact that it had already established that the provi-sions of the Data Protection Directive, in so far as they govern the pro-cessing of personal data liable to infringe fundamental freedoms, in par-ticular the right to privacy, must be interpreted in the light of funda-mental rights.[14] Given that Article 6 of the Directive requires controllers to keep personal data *'in a form which permits identification of data sub-jects for no longer than is necessary for the purposes for which the data were collected or for which they are further processed'*, a controller must take all reasonable steps to ensure that data which are processed in contraven-tion of this requirement are erased or rectified.[15]

---

13 Paragraph 87.
14 The Court cited cases *P Connolly v Commission CJEU C-274/99,* 6 March 2001, ECLI:EU:C:2001:127, and *Österreichischer Rundfunk and Others CJEU C-465/00,* 20 May 2003, ECLI:EU:C:2003:294.
15 Paragraph 72 of the *Google Spain* judgment.

The CJEU took Google Inc. to be processing the personal data on the basis of its business interests under the legal ground of legitimate interests (Article 7(f) of the Data Protection Directive).[16] This provision permits the controller to process personal data where it is necessary for a legitimate interest pursued by the controller or by third parties to whom the data is disclosed. A data subject is able to object to such processing, under Article 14 of the Directive, on *compelling legitimate grounds relating to his particular situation to the processing of data relating to him, save where otherwise provided by national legislation*. The economic interest of a search engine operator must be balanced against the data subject's fundamental rights.

On the aspect of the rights of other internet users the CJEU said the following:

> The processing of search engine results *'enables any internet user to obtain through the list of results a structured overview of the information relating to that individual that can be found on the internet — information which potentially concerns a vast number of aspects of his private life and which, without the search engine, could not have been interconnected or could have been only with great difficulty — and thereby to establish a more or less detailed profile of him. Furthermore, the effect of the interference with those rights of the data subject is heightened on account of the important role played by the internet and search engines in modern society, which render the information contained in such a list of results ubiquitous.'*[17]

According to the CJEU, the interest of other internet users must be balanced against the nature of the information that is in question, its sens-

---

16 Paragraph 73.
17 Paragraph 80.

itivity in relation to the data subject's private life, and the public interest.[18]

v   The 'right to be forgotten' (Question (6))

Mr Gonzalez argued that the fundamental rights to the protection of personal data and to privacy found in the Charter encompass the 'right to be forgotten' and override the legitimate interests of the search engine operator and the general interest in freedom of information. The court was also asked whether or not the information had to be 'prejudicial' to the data subject, even where lawfully published by third parties.

The CJEU, in considering this point, highlighted that even though the initial processing of personal data may be lawful and accurate, by Article 6(1)(c) to (e) of the Data Protection Directive, that processing may become incompatible with the Data Protection Directive over time where the processing of the data becomes inadequate, irrelevant, or excessive in relation to those initial purposes.[19] If this arises in the context of personal data that is processed for the purposes of providing search engine results, where processing under Article 7(f) is no longer justified, then the search engine operator must erase the information in the list.[20] The court added that it was not necessary to find that the information included in the search engine results list cause prejudice to the data subject.

As a rule, the CJEU said, the right of the data subject in this regard, and in the light of the Charter, override '*not only the economic interest of the operator of the search engine but also the interest of the general public in finding that information upon a search relating to the data subject's name*'.[21] However, there may be particular reasons, for example where the data subject has a role in public life or where making the informa-

---

18 Paragraph 81.
19 Paragraph 93.
20 Paragraph 94.
21 Paragraph 97.

tion available was in the public interest, that the interference with the data subject's fundamental rights is justified.[22]

Applying this approach to Mr Costeja's case, the CJEU found that the link to his name to online archives of a newspaper for an announcement that had taken place 16 years previously, and taking into account the sensitivity of that information, balanced against a limited interest in the public having access to that information, weighed in favour of its erasure.

Conclusion

The main points from the Google Spain judgment are:

1   The term 'establishment' is to be interpreted widely;

2   A search engine operator is processing personal data despite its ostensibly neutral function in relation to the content of the data;

3   A search engine operator is a controller of the personal data that it feeds into its search engine because it determines the purposes and means of the processing;

4   It is irrelevant that the personal data is lawfully processed by the original publisher of the content on its web page; and,

5   The legitimate ground for the processing of personal data by the search engine operator will need to be assessed in relation to the data subject's fundamental rights to privacy and data protection.

---

22 Ibid.

Although the CJEU in this case examined the situation under the Data Protection Directive, it is still applicable to the GDPR, and in particular clarifies the responsibility of a search engine website service. The EDPB recently published 'Guidelines 5/2019 on the criteria of the Right to be Forgotten in the search engines case under the GDPR (Part 1), adopted on 7 July 2010', which is examined in Chapter V.

The provisions referred to in the judgment

Article 2(b) of Data Protection Directive defines 'processing' of personal data and is equivalent to Article 4(2) of the GDPR.

Article 2(d) of the Data Protection Directive defines the 'controller' of personal data and is equivalent to Article 4(7) of the GDPR.

Articles 4(1)(a) and 4(1)(c) of the Data Protection Directive define the territorial scope of the Data Protection Directive. This has been expanded in the GDPR and can be found in Article 3 of the regulation.

Article 12(b) of the Data Protection Directive is the right of data subjects to obtain rectification, erasure or blocking of the data processing which does not comply with the Data Protection Directive. In the GDPR this has been divided into separate rights and can be found in Article 16 (rectification), Article 17 (erasure) and Article 18 (restriction).

Article 7(f) of the Data Protection Directive is the processing of personal data under legitimate interests and the GDPR equivalent is Article (6)(1)(f).

CHAPTER V

GUIDANCE FROM THE EUROPEAN DATA PROTECTION BOARD ON DELISTING

The EDPB recently published 'Guidelines on the right to be forgotten in the context of search engines and took into account the introduction of the GDPR since the *Google Spain* judgment'.[1] This chapter summarises the guidelines.

The right to delisting incorporates the right to object (GDPR Article 21) and the right to erasure (GDPR Article 17) and both can serve as a legal basis for a delisting request. Whilst these rights existed under the Data Protection Directive, the EDPB states that an 'adjustment' of the interpretation of the rights are required under the GDPR. The EDPB also clarified that GDPR Article 17 does not change the *Google Spain* judgment, but permits a data subject to make a delisting request under more than one ground.

The EDPB guidance makes clear that delisting does not erase the personal data completely, as the original source of the material – the media outlet, newspaper article, or website – will maintain control over it, even if it is no longer visible in search engine results based on a query related to the data subject's name. However, search engines still have a duty to erase the personal data to the extent that they control the data. '*In some exceptional cases*' the search engine operator may need to fully erase their indexes or caches, or fully erase the URL to the content if it were to stop respecting robots.txt requests implemented by the original publisher.[2]

---

1   EDPB 'Guidelines 5/2019 on the criteria of the Right to be Forgotten in the search engine cases under the GDPR (part 1)' adopted on 7 July 2020.

GDPR Article 17(2) – which places a duty on controllers to inform other controllers who are re-using the personal data that it has made public – does not apply to search engine operators in the context of delisting the personal data that has been indexed in a search result.[3] Search engine operators are also not obliged to inform the controller that is making the information public.[4] The EDPB is planning to publish further guidelines on GDPR Article 17(2) at a later date.

Delisting and Ground 1

This provision permits a data subject to request delisting where the personal data are no longer necessary in relation to the purposes for which they are being processed. For a search engine operator, the processing is carried out for the purposes of making the information easily accessible to internet users. Therefore in considering this ground the search engine operator must balance the protection of privacy of the data subject against the interests of internet users accessing the information. Whether or not the personal data has become out of date will be relevant to this assessment.

The EDPB gives the following examples for ground 1:

> ➢ Personal data held by a company that has been removed from the public register;

> ➢ A link to a company's website that contains contact details for the data subject even though he or she is no longer employed by the company;

---

2   A robots.txt file tells search engine crawlers which pages or files the crawler can or can't request from a website. They are usually used to keep a file or page from appearing on a search engine.

3   EDPB Guidelines 5/2019, ibid footnote 1, paragraph 12.

4   Ibid.

> ➢ Information that was published on the internet to meet a legal obligation, which has met its time limit.

Delisting and Ground 2

This ground is unlikely to apply to delisting, because the controller to whom the data subject gave consent is the web publisher, rather than the search engine operator. The consent referred to in ground 2 is specific to the GDPR, rather than some general concept of consent, and must relate to the processing activity carried out. This interpretation was endorsed by the CJEU in *GC and Others v Commission Nationale de l'Informatique et des Libertés*[5] (see Chapter VII). If the data subject makes an erasure request based on ground 2 to the web publisher, the publisher would be obliged under GDPR Article 17(2) to inform search engine operators who have indexed the data.

Delisting and Ground 3

The right to object constituted a ground to delist in the *Google Spain* judgment and was provided for by Article 14 of the Data Protection Directive. There are differences in the wording of Article 14 and its GDPR equivalent, Article 21. Under Article 14 the data subject had to demonstrate '*compelling legitimate grounds relating to his [or her] particular situation*' whereas under GDPR Article 21, the data subject has the right to object '*on grounds relating to his or her particular situation*' (my emphasis).

The GDPR has shifted the burden of proof onto the controller who must demonstrate 'compelling legitimate grounds for the processing' under Article 21(1) to be able to continue to process the personal data. Therefore where a search engine operator receives a request to delist

---

5 *CJEU Case C-136/17*, 24 September 2019, ECLI:EU:C:2019:773.

based on an objection due to the data subject's particular situation, it must erase the data unless it can demonstrate a legitimate ground that overrides the 'interests, rights and freedoms of the data subject'. This may include balancing the protection of privacy interests of internet users against the interests of internet users in accessing information.[6]

The EDPB states that the criteria for delisting developed by the Article 29 Working Party in 'Guidelines on the implementation of the Court of Justice of the European Union judgment on "Google Spain and Inc v. Agencia Española de Protección de Datos (AEPD) and Mario Costeja González" C-131/12' can still be used by search engine operators to assess a request for delisting under ground 3 (see the end of this chapter for a list of criteria from these guidelines).

A data subject's 'particular situation' must be carefully evaluated. Relevant criteria may be (but are not limited to):

> ➢ Detriment when applying for jobs;

> ➢ An impact on his or her personal reputation;

> ➢ Whether he or she has a role in public life;

> ➢ Whether the information at stake is related to his or her professional life or private life;

> ➢ If the information constitutes hate speech, slander, libel or similar offences;

> ➢ If the data is factually inaccurate;

> ➢ If the data relates to a minor criminal offence committed a long time ago which causes prejudice to the data subject.

---

6   Ibid., paragraph 30.

Note that the criteria above, or any other factors that relate to the 'particular situation', will not need to be examined unless there are compelling legitimate grounds on the part of the controller to refuse the request. The 'balancing' exercise only arises if those compelling legitimate grounds exist.

Delisting and Ground 4

The notion of unlawful processing shall be interpreted broadly in relation to delisting, such that the infringement of a legal provision other than the GDPR can also apply.[7] The interpretation '*must be conducted objectively by Supervisory Authorities, according to national laws or to a court decision*'. An example given, is where the listing of personal information is expressly prohibited by a court order.

Delisting and Ground 5

Compliance with a legal obligation includes that obligation to comply with an injunctive order, an express request by national or EU law for erasure, or a breach of the retention period of data.

Delisting and Ground 6

The EDPB highlights the difficulties in interpreting recital 18 of Directive 2000/31/EC[8] (the 'eCommerce Directive') which provides a definition of '*the direct provision of information society services*' that is

---

7   Ibid., paragraph 36.

8   'Of the European Parliament and of the Council of 8 June 2000 on certain legal aspects of information society services, in particular electronic commerce, in the Internal Market'.

both broad and ambiguous. Search engine operators' activities are likely to fall within the scope of the definition.

In the context of ground 6 however, search engine operators do not identify whether the personal data they are indexing concern an adult or a child. Whether or not the data subject is a child is relevant not only to ground 6, but also to the assessment of 'particular situation' in ground 3. The GDPR places special emphasis on children, and the fact that the data subject is a child means that they merit specific protection in regard to their personal data. The date at which the original processing of the data began will need to be known when evaluating this ground.

Delisting and Exemption 1

The CJEU in *Google Spain* distinguished between the legitimacy of a web publisher to disseminate information on the internet on the basis of a right to freedom of expression, and the legitimacy of the search engine provider to make available that information as part of its business operations. Nevertheless, '*the balance between protecting the rights of interested parties and freedom of expression, including free access to information, is an intrinsic part of Article 17 GDPR*'.[9] The ECtHR judgment in *ML and WW v Germany* indicates that the balancing of interests at issue may lead to different results.[10]

The rights of the data subjects to delisting must be weighed against the interests of internet users to access the information. That balance will depend upon the nature and context of the information in the specific case.[11] The EDPB concludes that, depending on the circumstances, a search engine provider may refuse to delist the content on the basis that

---

9   The EDPB Guidelines, paragraph 45.
10 ECtHR, application Nos 60798/10 and 65599/10, 28 June 2018.
11 The EDPB Guidelines, paragraph 47.

its listing is <u>strictly necessary</u> for protecting the freedom of information of internet users.[12]

Delisting and Exemption 2

Legal obligation

This exemption is less likely to apply to search engine operators. The scenario that the EDPB describes where it would be applicable, is the unlikely circumstance where Member State law enables a public authority to oblige search engine operators to publish information directly rather than through URL links to the web page where the information is found.[13]

Where the web publisher is under a legal obligation to maintain the information, the search engine operator cannot by extension rely on this legal obligation as an exemption to continue to list the personal data. However, the existence of the legal obligation on the web publisher will be relevant in assessing the balancing exercise described in exemption 1.

Public interest

Theoretically a search engine operator could carry out activities in the public interest if they were to be given authority by Member State law. The EDPB acknowledges that it is however highly unlikely that search engine operators would be used in this way to serve the public interest.

---

12 Ibid., paragraph 54.
13 Ibid., paragraphs 57 to 59.

Delisting and Exemption 3

The same conclusions were reached by the EDPB on exemption 3 as exemption 2 in application to search engine operators.

Delisting and Exemption 4

To rely on this exemption, the search engine provider must demonstrate that the delisting of content on the search result page (based on a name) poses a *'serious obstacle or completely prevents the achievement of scientific or historical research purposes of statistical purposes'*.[14] Whether or not the suppression of results could affect the research or statistical purposes of users of the search engine is not relevant for this exemption. Such a question is more appropriately considered in the balancing exercise described in exemption 1.

Delisting and Exemption 5

The EDPB does not add much on this exemption other than to state that it is unlikely to apply to search engine operators in the context of delisting, and that in any event, the information is suppressed as opposed to deleted by them.

---

14 Ibid., paragraph 79.

<u>Guidelines on the implementation of the Court of Justice of the European Union judgment on "Google Spain and Inc v. Agencia Española de Protección de Datos (AEPD) and Mario Costeja González" C-131/12', adopted 26 November 2014.</u>

Whilst these guidelines have not formally been adopted by the EDPB, they are still relevant in assessing delisting requests. The guidelines set out thirteen 'criteria', or questions, for data protection authorities to consider; further comment is provided in the guidelines in relation to each of these questions:

1. Does the search result relate to a natural person – i.e. an individual? And does the search result come up against a search on the data subject's name?

2. Does the data subject play a role in public life? Is the data subject a public figure?

3. Is the data subject a minor?

4. Is the data accurate?

5. Is the data relevant and not excessive?

    a. Does the data relate to the working life of the data subject?

    b. Does the search result link to information which allegedly constitutes hate speech/slander/libel or similar offences in the area of expression against the complainant?

    c. Is it clear that the data reflect an individual's personal opinion, or does it appear to be verified fact?

6. Is the information sensitive within the meaning of Article 8 of the Data Protection Directive?

7. Is the data up to date? Is the data being made available for longer than is necessary for the purpose of the processing?

8. Is the data processing causing prejudice to the data subject? Does the data have a disproportionately negative privacy impact on the data subject?

9. Does the search result link to information that puts the data subject at risk?

10. In what context was the information published?

    a. Was the content voluntarily made public by the data subject?

    b. Was the content intended to be made public? Could the data subject have reasonably known that the content would be made public?

11. Was the original content published in the context of journalistic purposes?

12. Does the publisher of the data have a legal power – or a legal obligation – to make the personal data publicly available?

13. Does the data relate to a criminal offence?

CHAPTER VI
PRACTICAL ISSUES

I. **Data Subjects**

<u>Identifying the Controller</u>

The first hurdle for a data subject is identifying the controller of the information that he or she wishes to be deleted or delisted, which may not be a straightforward task. Extensive data sharing between organisations has created a complex data ecosystem. For example, if you download an app, you agree to the terms and conditions. For the vast majority of apps, this means that once you use the app, your data is immediately shared with a number of third parties. Some may be for technical reasons so that the app can function, but the majority of apps also share the data with companies such as Google, Facebook and others.

The relationships between organisations sharing personal data can be unclear. Organisations may deflect responsibility to another organisation, on the basis that either they are merely processors, or that the specific data processing operation is not their responsibility. Under the GDPR, a processor is obliged to assist the controller in dealing with data subject access requests under Article 28(3)(e). However whilst a processor may inform the data subject that it has communicated the request to the controller, it is under no further obligation to assist the data subject.

Controllers are obliged to provide data subjects with information about the processing of their personal data, including the identity and contact details of the controller, and the recipients of the personal data under GDPR Articles 13 and 14. Where there are joint controllers of the information, the data subject can exercise their data rights against each of the controllers.[1] The controllers should inform each other if a deletion request is received, however it would be prudent for the data subject to make the request to each controller. A data subject may also request to the controller, that personal data processed by a processor on the controller's behalf is also deleted.

It can be difficult to find the location and source of the personal data placed on the internet. The Uniform Resource Locator 'URL' is the website address but it is not the source of the information. The homepage of a website may be stored in a directory that is located within a parent directory. The location of the personal data is not the homepage of the website, but in the parent directory. The source of the data is the person who uploaded the personal data onto the homepage of the website. A data subject – unless he or she decides to make a delisting request instead – will need to identify the controller and creator of the website page to make an erasure request. To find out who is hosting the website, a 'Whois' internet search will usually reveal the owner, or at least the administrative contact for the webmaster or the site's hosting company.

Subject Access Request

As set out in Chapter III, the right to erasure only applies under six specific grounds. In most situations a data subject will need to establish the data processing activities and purposes to make an effective erasure request, to engage one of the grounds. A controller may be performing various data processing operations on the personal data, potentially for different purposes, and under different legal bases. Unless the data subject has a clear picture of how the personal data is being used, it will be difficult to assert that a ground is made out. Further, it may be that a ground is engaged in respect to one processing operation, but not an-

---

1   GDPR Article 26(3).

other. It is important that a data subject is aware that the personal data may be deleted against one processing operation, but perhaps not all.

Under GDPR Article 15, a data subject has a right of access to his or her information. A controller is obliged to confirm whether or not personal data about him or her is being processed, and what that information is. Upon receiving a request under Article 15, the controller is also obliged to provide the data subject with information about:

- The purposes of the processing;

- The 'categories' of personal data that is being processed;

- Other controllers or third parties to whom the personal data already has, or will be, disclosed;

- Where possible, the envisaged period of time for which the personal data will be kept, or the criteria used to determine that period of time;

- The data subject rights that are available (rectification, erasure, restriction or objection);

- Information about the right to lodge a complaint with a supervisory authority;

- The source of the personal data, if not collected directly from the data subject; and,

- If relevant, the existence of any automated decision-making.

The controller must also provide a copy of the personal data that it holds.

A Request for Erasure

The data subject will need to put enough information in the erasure request to enable the controller to evaluate the request. The GDPR and the DPA 2018 do not specify what should be included in a notice to the controller exercising the right to be forgotten. As a minimum, a data subject should include:

> The identity of the controller and the date of the request;

> That the request is an erasure request as defined in Article 17 of the GDPR;

> The name of the requestor (and/or any information that the controller would be able to recognise the data subject e.g. if there is an account identification number, postal address etc.);

> How the data subject would like to be contacted by the controller and receive any information about the request (e.g. by email, post etc.);

> The personal data that the data subject wants to be erased;

> Which of the grounds in GDPR Article 17(1) the data subject seeks to rely on for the request; and,

> Whether the data subject wants other controllers of the data (and processors) to be informed of the erasure request.

There is no need to pre-empt reliance on one of the exemptions, or to show that the exemptions do not apply. However, where it is anticipated that the controller will rely on a particular exemption, it may expedite the process if a data subject were to provide enough detail for a controller to make an assessment. This is particularly important where the controller has to balance the data subject's 'particular situation' and or the 'risks to his or her rights and freedoms' against its own business interests. Whilst the data subject does not need to show harm in order to seek erasure, if the request is urgent for reasons of particular harm, the data subject should make this fact clear.

A Request for Delisting

Search engines have specific procedures for requests for delisting. Depending on the nature of the information that the data subject wishes to remove (or more accurately delist), it may be that the website operator, or search engine will remove it on the basis that it breaches the terms and conditions of the website or service. Given the constantly changing flow of information on the internet, and the speed at which postings or sites are moved or updated, it is advisable that data subjects take screenshots of the problematic webpages or material so that context can be provided when making a delisting request.

Whilst service providers and websites may have 'take down' or 'reporting' procedures in place, these are not to be confused with the right to erasure, as the former are linked to the company's policy or terms of service. The right to erasure is a distinct legal right, from which a company cannot opt out or restrict. If the content is removed from the website, it will no longer be found on search engines and social media sites.

Whilst a delisting request does not attract a charge and is therefore a costless starting point to try to restrict access to information from the internet, it is not a guarantee that the search engine will agree to remove all the URLs requested from the results. Google removes about half the URLs that are requested to be delisted.[2]

A delisting request is a request against an applicant's name. It does not remove search results that may appear where other information is put

---

2   See Google's transparency report.

into the search engine tool, other than a name, so that the same information may still easily appear. Data subjects should also be aware that the process is not quick, and they may need to seek an injunction from the court if the information needs to be removed from the internet urgently.

The *Google Spain* judgment shifted the responsibility onto search engines to assess whether or not a person has a right to be forgotten in relation to information made public about them. This is not a position that sits comfortably with most commercial organisations, who may consider that the courts are in a better position to make such assessments. Note that in Google's 'FAQ's – Privacy & Terms' it states the following:[3]

> *'In evaluating your request, we will look at whether the results include outdated information about your private life. We'll also look at whether there's a public interest in the information remaining in our search results – for example, if it relates to financial scams, professional malpractice, criminal convictions or your public conduct as a government official (elected or unelected). These are difficult judgements and as a private organisation, we may not be in a good position to decide on your case. If you disagree with our decision you can contact your local DPA.'*

Other Controllers and Internet Sources

As discussed in Chapter III, once a controller has determined that an effective erasure request has been made, it is obliged to inform other controllers of the request. Whether those other controllers do in fact delete the personal data is another matter. Their obligation to do so will de-

---

3   Accessed 20 September 2020.

pend on the legal basis they are using to process the personal data, and their compliance with data protection rules in relation to the processing. If the legal basis upon which they are processing the data for other purposes does not meet the criteria for any of the exemptions, then they will be obliged to erase the data as well.

Data subjects will need to be aware that information that is published online can be extremely difficult to erase completely. Delisting of results can be effective, because a search engine acts as a gateway for information; most people access information about others by typing their name into a search engine. However, the negative effects of personal data sharing may not be confined to search results, and the existence of other sources can cause particular problems.[4]

Data is constantly duplicated, sometimes using applications that controllers themselves may not be aware, especially if the original content has been posted publicly on the internet. This means that where a data subject may succeed in having the personal data deleted from one controller, it may appear elsewhere on the internet, provided by another controller.

Where the source of the information is determined that certain information is made public, it can be almost impossible to prevent it. Further, it is easy for information to become 'viral', where it is shared and republished at such speed, and to such an extent, that it is near impossible to stop. In *P and Q (Children: Care Proceedings: Fact Finding) [2015] EWFC 26 (19 March 2015)*, a mother and her partner uploaded videos of her children onto the internet, speaking about sexual abuse. The mother made accusations against the children's father, former teachers, professionals and other parents. The accusations were ultimately false.

---

4   See the examples given in oral evidence to the Parliamentary Joint Committee on Human Rights, 10 July 2019. One example is where a person was unable to secure banking or accounting services, as a result of a business intelligence report that documented the fact the person had been acquitted of a crime.

The mother and her partner had forced the children to invent allegations about a Satanic child abuse ring. The videos went viral and as of 10 March 2015, more than 4 million people had viewed the material online.[5]

Whilst YouTube will remove posts that are subject to an injunctive order, or breach the site's terms and conditions, it is still possible for individuals to create new accounts and continue to re-post the material. There are also automated archiving services such as 'Wayback Machine', 'Archive.org' and 'Google Cache' which may continue to make available webpages that have been deleted or delisted. It may be necessary to seek removal from these services as well.

Internet Intermediaries

Internet intermediaries, or hosting providers, are not liable for the information that they transmit or host. The eCommerce Directive defines an internet intermediary as:[6]

➤ A mere conduit (Article 12)

➤ A caching service provider (Article 13)

➤ A hosting service provider (Article 14)

Article 1(5)(b) of the eCommerce Directive states that it does not apply to *'questions relating to information society services covered by Directives 95/46/EC and 97/66/EC'*, excluding it from the data protection framework. However, according to GDPR Article 2(3), the regulation applies without prejudice to the eCommerce Directive. In the UK, the Elec-

---

5 *P and Q (Children: Care Proceedings: Fact Finding)*, paragraph 2.
6 Directive 2000/31 of the European Parliament and of the Council of 8 June 2000 on certain legal aspects of information society services, in particular electronic commerce, in the Internal Market.

tronic Commerce (EC Directive) Regulations 2002 implements the eCommerce Directive.

A key question is whether or not a data subject can invoke his or her data protection rights against an internet intermediary or hosting site of information that has been uploaded for a third party. This can be important if the data subject is unable to identify the third party to be able to seek an erasure request. The CJEU cases of *C-236/08 to C-238/08*[7] and *Case 324/09*[8] imply that an intermediary that falls into the definition of the eCommerce Directive is more likely to be considered a processor rather than a controller. However if the intermediary is also processing the personal data for its own business activities (such as in *Google Spain*) then it will more likely be concluded to be a controller.

The Household Exception

An issue that arises for many individuals who are facing problems with information that is being made public is that the source may be from a person as opposed to an organisation or company. Where the information is in the control of a person, it may be that the GDPR does not apply because of the household exception (discussed in Chapter III). The exception is however interpreted narrowly. In the CJEU case of *Bodil Lindqvist v Åklagarkammaren i Jönköping*[9] a church volunteer who had created a website for parishioners that included personal data of fellow volunteers was found not to fall within the exception.

---

7   *Google France SARL and Google Inc. v Louis Vuitton Malletier SA, Google France SARL v Viaticum SA and Luteciel SARL, Google France SARL v Centre national de recherche en relations humaines (CNRHH) SARL and Others, 23 March 2010*

8   *L'Oreal v eBay, 12 July 2011.*

9   *CJEU Case C101-01, 6 November 2003, ECLI:EU:C:2003:596.*

In *Lindqvist*, the CJEU clarified the scope of the household exemption finding that there are two criteria:[10]

(i) The activities need to be carried out in the course of the person's private or family life; and,

(ii) The data cannot be made available to an indefinite number of people.

Attorney General AG Tizzano, in his Opinion on the case, concluded that the household exception will not be applicable where the personal data is loaded *'on a home page accessible by anyone, anywhere in the world, through a specific link on a site well-known to the public (and therefore easy to find with a search engine)'*.[11] The CJEU similarly found the household exception did not apply in the case of *František Ryneš v Úřad pro ochranu osobních údajů*,[12] where video surveillance was used by a household at its front door, because it monitors a public space.

The application of this can be seen in practice. Recently in Holland, a grandmother who was posting photographs of her grandchildren on social media without their parent's consent, was found not to be exempt from the GDPR.[13] The court was influenced by the fact that the posting on social media made the photographs available to a large audience.

Where the household exception applies to the person who is making available information, thereby exempting the disclosure from the data protection regime, it still may be possible to seek delisting of it on the basis it breaches the terms and conditions of the search engine, or service. If that is unsuccessful, or even before such a solution is pursued, it may also be possible to bring a privacy claim against the person.

---

10 Ibid., paragraph 47.
11 *CJEU Advocate Opinion Case C101-01*, 19 September 2002, ECLI:EU:C:2002:513, paragraph 34.
12 *CJEU Case C-212/13*, 11 December 2014, ECLI:EU:C:2014:2428.
13 Rb. Gelderland – C/05/368427, 13 May 2020.

Other Legal Claims

There are potential alternative causes of action in a situation where information is having a consequential effect on a person. For claims in harassment, misuse of private information, breach of confidence or defamation it is possible to get a permanent injunction. These areas of law go beyond the scope of this book, but it is important to be aware that these legal options may be more suitable to the facts of the case, or more effective in outcome.

It may also be possible in some circumstances to seek removal of information from a search engine's listing results not through a right to be forgotten request, but on the basis that it does not meet the company's policy or terms of service. For example, Google will remove material that creates significant risks of identity theft, or financial fraud. It will also remove sensitive medical or national identification material, involuntary fake pornography, 'doxxing'[14] content, or explicit personal images.

II. Controllers

Time Limit to Respond

There is a relatively short time limit to respond to a data subject. According to GDPR Article 12(3), a controller shall provide information on request under Articles 15 to 22 *without undue delay and in any event within one month of receipt of the request*. Whilst it is possible to seek an extension by two further months, *'where necessary'*, this is not an option to be used simply to gain more time. There must be a particular complexity that makes the extension necessary.

---

14 The publication of identifying information in the context of harassing, shaming, extorting or otherwise in a manner that is 'vigilante' in nature.

Time starts to run from the day the controller receives the request, or the day the controller verifies the identity of the data subject (if later). One month is calculated as the corresponding calendar date in the next month, or if the next month is shorter (i.e. no corresponding date is possible), then it will be the end of the month. If the corresponding date falls on a weekend or bank holiday, the last day is taken as the next working day.

Given the short timeframe for response it is advisable that controllers have considered in advance how they will deal with a request for erasure and put in place appropriate procedures, processes and training. When establishing policies and procedures controllers should consider the nature of the personal data they process, the potential consequences of the processing of the personal data, and the potential adverse effects on individuals.

Controllers should also decide how they will communicate such requests to joint controllers, processors and other controllers of the personal data and have procedures in place. Note that it is not possible to charge a fee to comply with a subject access request, unless it is 'manifestly unfounded or excessive' or an individual requests further copies after the controller has satisfied the request.

Clarifying the Request

If the controller is uncertain that it has received an erasure request it should seek clarification before deleting the personal data. If there are consequential effects on the data subject from the deletion of the personal data it would be prudent to explain the outcome, as it may not be obvious to the data subject making the request.

The controller must respond to the request for erasure if it is made, and not interpret the request as a different data subject right. It may be that the controller requires more information to be able to respond to the request, but the ICO makes clear that this does not extend the time for responding to the claim. Further, a controller may not ask the data subject to narrow the scope of his or her request, but may ask for additional details to assist in the search for the information.

The Refusal Notice

A refusal notice should include reasons why the grounds relied on for an erasure request do not apply, or why an exemption applies. GDPR Article 12(4) obliges the controller to inform the data subject of the reasons for not taking action, and also of the right to lodge a complaint with a data supervisory authority or making a claim in court.

Time Limit for Deletion

GDPR Article 17(1) states that a controller shall erase personal data *'without undue delay'* where one of the grounds is met, and no exemptions apply. A precise amount of time is not specified, but it is likely given the wording in recital 59 and Article 12(3) that the latest is one month, unless there are good reasons why it would take longer (see below 'technical issues'). The wording of Article 17(1) also implies that there are two time limits. First, the controller has up to one month to respond to the erasure request, and then it has another month to delete the data.

Where the reasons for the request are due to particular harm to the data subject as a consequence of the availability of the personal data, the controller should delete it as a matter of urgency. For example, where a data subject is experiencing online abuse, or harassment.

<u>Informing Controllers</u>

The controller is obliged to inform other controllers with whom the data has been shared of the erasure request (see Chapter III). However, if this *'proves impossible or involves disproportionate effort'* the controller is exempt but must inform the data subject that it cannot do so, and give details of the recipients that have not been notified.[15]

<u>Keeping Records</u>

In most scenarios, the controller will be processing personal data for multiple purposes. For example, an online retailer will use a person's name to send the item to the person, to process payment and will also most likely keep a record of that person's name for their business records.

Even where a valid erasure request has been made it will be necessary for controllers to keep a record of the request, and the action taken, in order to show compliance should there be a dispute at a later date. Controllers need to consider all aspects of their processing activities in relation to the data upon which an erasure request is made and inform the data subject of such records kept.

<u>The Legal Basis</u>

If they have not already done so, controllers should review the legal basis of the personal data they collected or received before the GDPR came into effect. If relying on consent, they should bear in mind that under the Data Protection Directive, consent was not equivalent to GDPR consent. Where the consent upon which the data was collected does not meet the GDPR standard, then not only does ground 2 not

---

15 GDPR Article 19.

apply, but ground 4 is met, as the data is being unlawfully processed. The burden is on the controller to show that it has obtained valid consent.[16]

There are certain 'rules' that controllers should be aware of:

(1) It is not possible to 'switch' a legal basis for processing at a later date. That is, a controller cannot rely on consent when it collects the data for processing for a particular purpose, and then 'switch' to legitimate interest.

(2) There cannot be more than one legal basis that applies to the same processing action, although there can be more than one legal basis that applies to the personal data where there are multiple processing actions. For example, the online retailer processes a person's name to send them an item (contract), and also processes the person's name when keeping a record of the transaction (legitimate interest).

If relying on the legal ground of legitimate interest a controller may be asked by the data subject to show how it balanced the interests of the data subject against its own legitimate interest for it to be valid. A legitimate interests assessment document is often used by controllers to be able to show that this legal ground is valid, and to comply with the principle of accountability. The ICO has a template on its website. This will be particularly important if the data subject is relying on ground 3 or ground 4 (where the legal basis is legitimate interest) to request erasure.

---

16 GDPR Article 7 and recital 42.

Purpose(s) of the Processing

To assess whether or not an exemption is engaged from the application of a data subject right, it is necessary to identify the purpose(s) for which the personal data is being processed and by whom. Where a processor or controller is processing personal data for a different set of purposes, each will need to be examined to see if a ground or an exemption applies. As mentioned earlier, it may be that there is a valid request in relation to some data processing operations but not to others. It would be wise to explain this clearly to the data subject and provide information as required by GDPR Articles 13 and 14 on the remaining processing operations.

Joint Control, Sharing Data and Liability

GDPR Article 82 provides for the right to compensation and liability; compensation is discussed in Chapter VIII. According to Article 82(4), where more than one controller or processor are involved in the processing of personal data, they shall be jointly liable for any damage caused by the processing. Where controllers are 'joint controllers' for the purposes of GDPR Article 26, the arrangements between them must be made available to the data subject. The data subject can enforce its data rights against either controller, irrespective of the arrangement between the controllers. A processor will only be liable to the extent that it has breached its obligations as a processor, or where it has acted outside of its instructions from the controller.[17]

The assessment of joint control is not always straightforward given the complicated commercial relationships that exist in the use of personal data. In the CJEU case *Unabhangiges Landeszentrum fur Datenschutz Schleswig-Hostein v Wirtschaftsakademie Schleswig-Holstein GmbH* it was decided that a controller is determined by fact rather than a formal ana-

---

17 GDPR Article 82(2).

lysis.[18] In *Wirtschaftsakademie* the administrators of a 'Facebook' fan page were concluded to be joint controllers with Facebook Inc., even though they did not have access to the original data and only anonymised statistics about demographics. This was because they decided how the processing was performed in relation to the visitors of the webpage. The point in issue was so-called 'web tracking', which is where internet users are tracked by companies through the websites they visit via 'cookies', to build a picture, or profile, on their interests and habits. Neither Wirtschaftsakademie, nor Facebook, had informed the visitors to the fan page that Facebook collected and subsequently processed their personal data.

In the case of *Fashion ID GmbH & Co. KG v Verbraucherzentrale NRW eV*, the CJEU ruled that websites that embed social platform 'sharing' or 'like' buttons could also be joint controllers.[19] The existence of these so-called 'social plugins' on a website means that every time an internet user goes to the website, whether or not they click on the 'share' or 'like' button, their IP address is sent to Facebook. The consumer protection association Verbrauchzentrale NRW brought a claim against the retailer on the basis that visitors of the site had not been informed of, or given their consent to, this form of personal data sharing.

Controllers should evaluate their data sharing arrangements, and where those arrangements indicate a relationship of joint control, ensure they have determined how each controller will address an erasure request and how liability will be apportioned.

---

18 *CJEU Case C-210/16*, 5 June 2018, ECLI:EC:C:2018:388. See also *Tieto Tietosuojavaltuutettu v Jehovan todistajat CJEU Case C-25/17*, 10 July 2018, ECLI:EU:C:2018:551.

19 *CJEU Case C-40/17*, 29 July 2019, ECLI:EU:C:2019:629.

III. General

Criminal Conviction Data

Personal data relating to criminal convictions and offences are afforded special protection in the GDPR and the DPA 2018. Article 10 of the GDPR specifies that the processing of such personal data '*shall be carried out only under the control of official authority or when the processing is authorised by Union or Member State law providing for appropriate safeguards for the rights and freedoms of data subjects*'.

In the UK, the Rehabilitation of Offenders Act 1974 ('ROA 1974') penalises the unauthorised disclosure of 'spent convictions'. A person who has been rehabilitated, and their conviction 'spent', is to be treated as a person who has not been convicted. In general, they are not obliged to reveal the conviction to a potential employer and should not be dismissed from employment or a profession or prejudiced in any way by failing to do so.[20]

Whether or not a conviction is spent may influence a delisting, or right to be forgotten request. In *MM v The United Kingdom* the ECtHR found that a spent conviction or caution becomes a part of a person's private life as it recedes into the past, and this can be a factor in the assessment of whether or not such information should be forgotten.[21] Google states in its policy that its approach to spent convictions, exonerations, and acquittals is to favour delisting of such results, and it will consider its nature and date.

However, it is unlikely that a challenge to a record of a conviction, investigation or caution processed by the police or an official public body

---

20 Some professions are exempt, most notably those that require a standard or enhanced DBS criminal record checks.

21 *Application No. 24029/07 (13 November 2012)*, paragraph 188. See also the ECtHR case of *ML and WW v Germany [2018] ECHR 554*.

is likely to be successful. In *Chief Constable of Humberside v Information Commissioner and another [2009] EWCA Civ 1079,* a request to delete minor convictions was refused and the Court of Appeal found that such data retention was in the public interest in preventing crime.

See also Chapter VII of this book.

Metadata

Controllers may make a distinction between data that is collected directly from the data subject, and data that it collects, infers or analyses from the data subject's activity or use of its service. This latter category is known as 'metadata'. Examples include device information, a log of information related to a data subject's activity, the time and date of the creation of data.

Whilst the GDPR does not specify rules for metadata, some are likely to come within the description of an online identifier in recital 30 of the GDPR, or the broad definition of personal data within Article 4(1). In some circumstances metadata could be personal data because it can be used with other information to identify an individual.

In the case of *Patrick Breyer v Bundesrepublik Deutschland*[22] the CJEU ruled that dynamic IP addresses are capable of being 'personal data' for the purposes of the Data Protection Directive. Breyer had brought an action against the Federal Republic of Germany for storing his IP address after he had visited government websites aimed at providing information to the public, arguing that it was unnecessary once he was no longer using the website. The court agreed, concluding that his dynamic IP address could be combined with information held by the internet service provider to identify him, and that the data controller in

---

22 *CJEU Case C-582/14,* 19 October 2016, ECLI:EU:C:2016:779.

the case (the German government) had the lawful means to obtain that information.

It is therefore possible for a data subject to make an erasure request of metadata held on him or her, if one of the grounds in GDPR Article 17(1) is met. It is important to be aware that controllers may not themselves classify metadata as personal data, and it may be necessary to specify the types of metadata or information that is the subject of the request. For example, Google (according to its privacy policy) makes a distinction between the data the data subject has provided to it, and the information that it receives or infers from the data subject's use of its data.

Facebook does the same and divides the data it processes into:

1. Things you do and information you provide

2. Things others do and information they provide

3. Information from third-party partners

4. Your networks and connections

5. Device information

Anonymised Data

The GDPR does not apply to personal data that has been anonymised. This is defined in recital 26 as *'information which does not relate to an identified or identifiable natural person or data rendered anonymous in such a way that the data subject is not or no longer identifiable'*. Whether or not anonymisation has actually been achieved involves an assessment of *'all the means reasonably likely to be used, such as singling out, either by the controller or by another person to identify the natural person directly or indirectly.'*[23] This involves the consideration of all objective factors, including the cost, the time taken to re-identify the data, the available technology and any technological developments.

Where a controller has anonymised personal data, the data will no longer be subject to data protection rules. In any event, it will not be possible to locate the data to be able to erase it. For example Apple's 'Siri' function, which records voice data in order to deliver the service, is unable to re-link the voice data back to the individual.[24]

Location Data

Location data can reveal particularly sensitive information about a person. From the places visited and the mapping of locations on particular days it can be possible to make conclusions about a person's employment, religion, health or other characteristic. The global debate about the issue of privacy in the use of Covid-19 tracing apps highlights the concerns people have about the collection of their location data. Location data can be personal data that could be subject to a request for erasure.

The ePrivacy Directive governs traffic, location and electronic communications content data. The ePrivacy Directive is considered *lex generalis* of the GDPR, which means that it will take precedence over the GDPR where there are specific obligations in connection with the provision of publicly available electronic communications services.

The ePrivacy Directive will at some point be replaced by the ePrivacy Regulation, which has been undergoing many years of debate. That debate goes beyond the scope of this book, but it is important to bear in mind that the rules will at some point change. To make an erasure re-

---

23 GDPR recital 26.
24 See: https://www.apple.com/uk/privacy/

quest of location data it will also be necessary to consider the provisions of the ePrivacy Directive, and domestic legislation that implements it in the Member State. It is uncertain as yet what law will apply in the UK post-Brexit, but at present the Privacy and Electronic Communications (EC Directive) Regulations 2003 is the relevant law, which implements the ePrivacy Directive.

Technical Issues

From a practical perspective, it may be difficult to erase personal data due to technical reasons. For example the technical infrastructures used in the context of internet security systems may not permit granular erasure. There may also be cached copies of the data stored on local disks of other computers, back-up copies, or archived and cached copies stored elsewhere. The personal data may also be retrievable from physical locations such as flash disk devices and USB sticks, smart phones, notebooks and other electronic devices. Deleting files from these devices does not prevent recovery of the data from the device, which can be done using readily available technical means.[25] The only absolute guarantee of deletion is the physical destruction of these devices.[26] Where the controller is only able to de-activate, archive, or 'put beyond use' the personal data, it should inform the data subject of this fact.[27]

---

25 See the European Network and Information Security Agency, 'The Right to be Forgotten – between expectations and practice', 10/18/2011.

26 See the ICO's guidance 'Deleting personal data', 26 February 2014. Available: https://ico.org.uk/media/for-organisations/documents/1475/deleting_personal_data.pdf

27 Ibid.

CHAPTER VII
THE RIGHT TO BE FORGOTTEN IN THE COURTS

There are three important cases involving the right to be forgotten of which to be aware. The first is the UK case of *NT1 & NT2 v Google LLC (the Information Commissioner intervening) [2018] EWHC 799 (QB)* in the High Court. The second is *GC and Others v Commission nationale de l'informatique et des libertés C-136/17* in the CJEU,[1] which considered the lawfulness of processing of sensitive data by a search engine operator. The third is *Google LLC v Commission nationale de l'informatique et des libertés C-507/17*,[2] in which the CJEU determined the territorial scope of the right to be forgotten.

NT1 & NT2 v Google LLC

NT1 was a businessman who had been involved in a controversial business that offered services and credit to consumers and companies in connection with property, and who was sentenced to a term of imprisonment for an accounting conspiracy related to the business in the late 1990s. NT1 was also accused of, but not tried for, a separate conspiracy connected with the same business. There were a number of successful civil claims brought against the business, and the fallout was subject to comments in Parliament. NT1 transferred substantial amounts from the business into offshore companies before it was compelled to wind-up.

---

1   24 September 2019, ECLI:EU:C:2019:773.
2   24 September 2019, ECLI:EU:C:2019:772.

In 2014, NT1 made a delisting request to Google LLC ('Google') to remove links to media articles related to his criminal conviction; at the time of his request his conviction was 'spent' under the ROA 1974. Google agreed to remove one link but refused to delist the remaining five. NT1 brought legal proceedings, seeking the blocking and/or erasure of links to media reports and a book extract, an injunction to prevent Google continuing to return to such links, and financial compensation.

NT2 had been involved in a business that was publicly criticized for its environmental practices. Various protestors had targeted the business and NT2 had received death threats. He authorised an investigations firm to use phone tapping and computer hacking to find the culprits. These activities were later discovered by the authorities. He was prosecuted but pleaded guilty to two counts of conspiracy at an early stage in the proceedings. NT2 received a short custodial sentence of six months. The conviction became 'spent' several years before the delisting request.

NT2 wished to remove links on the internet to reports of his conviction that appeared against his name in a Google search and made a request in 2015. Google refused. He sought the same remedies as NT1.

The main issues that Mr Justice Warby considered were:

1   Whether the claimant is entitled to the links being delisted either (a) because they are inaccurate, or (b) because they present an an unjustified interference with the claimant's data protection and/or privacy rights;

2   If so, whether the claimant is entitled to compensation.

The claimants argued that the processing by Google of their personal data, to produce search results listings that linked them to items that revealed their convictions, breached section 4(4) DPA 1998 in that the information was 'inaccurate' and 'maintained for longer than is necessary for a conceivable legitimate purpose'.[3] They further argued that none of the conditions in Schedule 2 and 3 that would allow Google to lawfully process sensitive data were met. The claimants sought blocking and/or erasure under sections 10 and 14 DPA 1998.

In its defence, Google relied on the 'journalism, literature and art' exemption in Part III section 32 DPA 1998. In relation to both claimants, Google argued that the information was accurate and that there was a public interest in maintaining the links to the articles that meant the processing was both legitimate and necessary for its purpose, in compliance with the *Google Spain* ruling.

In relation to NT1, Google had taken into account the following in its decision not to delist the information:

> ➤ NT1 has a subsequent business career that brings him into the public domain;

> ➤ NT1's business career has involved using the money he had profited from the conspiracy;

> ➤ NT1 continued to obstruct the Inland Revenue after his conviction;

> ➤ NT1 had created an online profile that was misleading and dishonest.

In relation to NT2, Google had taken into account the following:

> ➤ NT2 is currently involved in a business in property, and sports marketing and there remains a public interest in knowing about his past, in particular for those who might become involved or affected by his current business;

---

3   See paragraph 24 of the judgment.

> ➤ NT2 has made public statements about his conviction in interviews with the national media to 'exculpate' any damage to his reputation.

Spent Convictions

The fact that the information related to criminal offences was the key issue.[4] It was relevant that for the purposes of the ROA 1974 the claimants' sentences were spent at the time of trial. The purpose of the act is to rehabilitate offenders by protecting them from prejudicial treatment related to their convictions. However, according to section 8 ROA 1974, former convicts cannot obtain remedies for injury to their reputation from the publication in good faith of accurate information about a spent conviction. This can be interpreted to include an action in data protection and/or misuse of private information.[5]

Warby J made the following points in relation to the issue of spent convictions and privacy:

- The right to rehabilitation is an aspect of the law of personal privacy, which includes the right to reputation, the right to respect for family life and private life, but it is not unqualified;[6]

- The starting point is that a person does not enjoy a reasonable expectation of privacy in relation to information disclosed in legal proceedings held in public, but over time this may change;[7]

---

4   And relevant to criteria 13 in the Article 29 Working Party's guidelines.
5   See paragraph 166 (of the NT1 & NT2 judgment).
6   Ibid.
7   Ibid., paragraph 48.

- It is possible that a conviction may become an aspect of an individual's private life and so within the ambit of Article 8 of the Convention;[8]

- Information about a conviction, whether spent or not, is not confidential information;[9]

- The fact that a conviction is spent will be a 'weighty' but not definitive factor against further use or disclosure of the information;

- The particular circumstances and rights asserted by the offender will need to be evaluated and weighed against any competing right to freedom of speech, or other relevant factors.

There were particular factors that led Warby J to draw different conclusions on NT1 and NT2 and the relevance of their convictions, even though both were spent. NT1 had been convicted of a serious offence of dishonesty, to which he had been convicted at trial. Warby J noted that the trial judge had found that NT1 was *'the boss who had to shoulder the major share of the blame for the dishonesty conspiracy'*.[10] NT1 did not give evidence at the criminal trial and had appealed unsuccessfully against conviction. He received a sentence of four years' of imprisonment and was disqualified from acting as a company director. Warby J found NT1's evidence to be unsatisfactory, in particular that he did

---

8   See *R(L) v Comr of Police for the Metropolis (Secretary of State for the Home Dept intervening) [2010] 1 AC 310; R(T) v Chief Constable of Greater Manchester Police [2015] AC 49; Gaughran v Chief Constable for the Police Service of Northern Ireland [2016] AC 345; CG v Facebook Ireland Ltd [2017] EMLR 12; R(P) v Secretary of State for the Home Department [2017] 2 Cr App R12.*

9   See *Elliott v Chief Constable of Wiltshire (The Times, 5 December 1996), L v Law Society [2008] EWCA Civ 811.*

10   Ibid., paragraph 74.

not acknowledge his guilt in relation to the conviction and had '*tended to evade, to exaggerate, to obfuscate, and worse*' in the witness box.[11] NT1's conviction, whilst spent, was '*at the very outer limit of the statutory scheme*' and would never have been spent had it not been for amendments to the law made in 2014.[12]

NT2 on the other hand had been convicted of an invasion of privacy crime as opposed to one involving dishonesty, for which he had admitted making '*a cataclysmic mistake*'.[13] Warby J had found NT2 to be '*an honest and generally reliable witness*'.[14] He accepted that NT2's motivations for committing the offence were to identify those responsible for trespass, criminal damage and death threats to bring them to justice, and not for any personal financial gain. Google's case that NT2 had been trying to prevent legitimate protest was rejected. NT2 had also pleaded guilty at an early opportunity and did not seek to appeal against his sentence; he was sentenced to six months' imprisonment.

Data Inaccuracy

The claimants contended that some of the content that appeared in Google's search engine listing against their names breached the fourth principle of the DPA 1998: that the personal data is accurate. Warby J referred to the Article 29 Working Party's 'Guidelines on the implementation of the Court of Justice of the European Union judgment on "Google Spain and Inc v. Agencia Española de Protección de Datos (AEPD) and Mario Costeja González" C-131/12'. He noted the comments on criterion 4:

---

11 Ibid., paragraph 91.
12 Ibid., paragraph 167.
13 Ibid., paragraph 203.
14 Ibid., paragraph 176.

'In general, 'accurate' means accurate as to a matter of fact. There is a difference between a search result that clearly relates to one person's opinion of another person and one that appears to contain factual information....DPA's will be more likely to consider that de-listing of a search result is appropriate where there is inaccuracy as to a matter of fact and where this presents an inaccurate, inadequate or misleading impression of an individual'.

Warby J was of the view that the law of defamation can assist in considering whether or not words create a 'misleading impression of an individual' for the purposes of the inaccuracy test. He highlighted the 'repetition rule' in defamation that recognises that an accurate report by a third party may convey an inferential meaning that is false. Warby J made the point that whilst data protection law and defamation law are not 'co-terminous', it is appropriate to bear in mind domestic principles to ensure coherence in the law.[15]

He was critical of the fact that NT1 had not adequately stated his case in relation to inaccuracy, or provided evidence to support the claim. In relation to some of the items, NT1 complained that they created the false impression that he had been convicted of the second conspiracy, but Warby J concluded that overall a clear account had been given of his actual crime. All NT1's claims of inaccuracy were rejected on the basis that they represented contemporaneous reporting of his conviction, the civil claims brought against his company and the decisions of courts in relation to these events.

NT2 however was more successful on this point. Warby J drew on defamation principles to conclude that *'a person is referred to, or identifiable, if the words complained of would be taken by a reasonable reader of*

---

15 Paragraph 87 (of the NT1 & NT2 judgment).

the article or item as a whole to refer to the claimant'.[16] He concluded that the article complained of gave a misleading portrayal of the claimant's criminality and conveyed imputations that amounted to inaccuracy for the purposes of data protection. It is difficult to make a thorough assessment of the application of the law to the facts because Warby J set out his reasons for finding the article complained of as inaccurate in a private judgment so as not to reveal the identity of NT2.

The 'Journalism' Exemption

Section 32 DPA 1998 applies to processing of personal data for 'special purposes', which includes processing encompassing 'journalism, literature and art'. The effect of the section is to exempt processing for the special purposes from section 10 (processing likely to cause damage or distress) and 14 (rectification, blocking, erasure and destruction) of the DPA 1998.

The issue was whether or not section 32 was engaged at all. The wording of section 32(1) is as follows: '*personal data which are processed only for the special purposes…*' (my emphasis). Warby J found that Google failed at the threshold stage on this point, because it could not be said that the concept of 'journalism' is so broad as to include activities involving the disclosure of information to the public.[17] Section 32(1)(a) describes processing '*with a view to the publication by any person of any journalistic, literary or artistic material*'. Reliance on this subsection was rejected, on the basis that it could only narrowly apply to third parties who published the information solely for journalistic, or other, special purposes. It would be incidental to Google's primary commercial purpose of providing automated access to information indexed by its algorithm.[18]

---

16 Ibid., paragraph 189.
17 Ibid., paragraph 98.
18 Ibid., paragraphs 99 and 100.

Reliance on subsections 32(1)(b) and (c) were also unsuccessful:

> '*The data controller must establish that it held a belief that publication would be in the public interest, and that this belief was objectively reasonable; it must establish a subjective belief that compliance with the provision from which it seeks exemption would be incompatible with the special purposes in question, and that this was an objectively reasonable belief... There is no evidence that anyone at Google ever gave consideration to the public interest in continued publications of the URLs complained of, at any time before NT1 complained'.*[19]

DPA Compliance

Warby J rejected Google's reliance on condition 6(c) in Schedule 3 DPA 1998. In his view the processing could not be said to be necessary for the purpose of exercising legal rights in the context of Google's business rights under Article 16 of the Charter, or those rights related to internet users under Article 10 of the Convention and Articles 8 and 11 of the Charter. The judge found condition 5 in Schedule 3 was however satisfied so as to permit the processing of sensitive personal data. That is, that the claimants had made the personal data public *'as a result of steps deliberately taken by the data subject'*.[20] He rejected the argument that the steps taken must be in relation to information, stating *'a person who deliberately conducts himself in a criminal fashion runs the risk of apprehension, prosecution, trial, conviction, and sentence. Publicity for what happens at trial is the ordinary consequence of the open justice principle.'*[21]

---

19 Ibid., paragraph 102.
20 Ibid., paragraph 110 and 111.
21 Ibid., paragraph 111.

A condition in schedule 2 must also be met for the processing to be 'fair and lawful'. It was found that Google clearly has a legitimate interest in the processing of third party data as it is a fundamental part of its business operations. Third parties also had a legitimate interest in receiving information from Google or other internet search engines. The ultimate question is whether the processing is necessary for these legitimate interests. According to Warby J, this involved a balancing exercise that was described in *Google Spain* and is essentially equivalent to the Article 8/Article 10 'ultimate balance test' as prescribed by *Murray v Express Newspapers [2007] EWHC 1908 (Ch)*. It also involves scrutiny of the comparative importance of the specific rights in the case, including the right to freedom of information in Article 11 of the Charter.[22]

Public Life

Warby J found that the protection of reputation was the substantial motivation in requesting the delistings, but that there were factors for both NT1 and NT2 that involved areas of their private lives. The authorities support the proposition that injury to reputation can engage Article 8 of the Convention .[23] In the commentary to criteria 5 in the Article 29 Working Party's guidelines, it was noted that a distinction is made between a person's private life and their public or professional 'persona'. A key question is whether or not the public is protected against improper public or professional conduct by having access to particular information.

Whilst NT1's controversial business had made him reasonably well known to the public in the 1990s, his post-conviction business had been limited to commercial lending, for which he did not deal with

---

22 Ibid., paragraph 132.

23 See *McKennitt v Ash [2006] EWCA Civ 1714 [2008] QB 73, Gulati v MGN Ltd [2015] EWHC 1482 (Ch), Khuja v Times Newspaper Ltd [2017] UKSC 49 [2017] 3 WLR 351.*

consumers. Warby J accepted that his current business position was no longer 'prominent' compared with the decade before. However, NT1 had taken steps to 'correct' his online profile by engaging the services of a reputation management business that created 'positive' internet postings about his credentials. These postings *clearly promote[d] the idea that NT1 is a man of unblemished integrity, with a longstanding reputation as such* and were aimed at the public.[24]

NT2 was found to have a minor role in public life, and that in this regard it was relevant that the crime he was convicted of was one involving privacy and not dishonesty. As such Warby J found that the relevance of his conviction to his interactions with investors, staff, customers or businesses was *'slender to non-existent'*.[25] Further his public interviews did not contradict his past or make false claims: he had admitted the prosecution's allegations. The interviews NT2 gave to the media had been based on his consent. Warby J said that no particular circumstances had been identified to make it legitimate to continue to process the personal data now that he had withdrawn his consent.[26]

Harm or Prejudice

Whilst a data subject need not prove prejudice or harm, where there is evidence of such harm, it would be a weighty factor in favour of delisting. NT1 did not provide much evidence to describe the particular harm or prejudice that the availability of the publications had caused. Warby J noted the lack of evidence to show how many searches have been, or were being made, against his name. He had described damage and distress in his particulars of claim as follows: treatment as a pariah in his personal, business and social life; threats made in public; disruption of family life. The judge concluded these to be legitimate, but that

---

24 Paragraphs 124 and 130 (of the NT1 & NT2 judgment).
25 Ibid., paragraph 204.
26 Ibid., paragraph 220.

on the evidence (there were no witness statements from family members), it appeared that NT1's main concern was his business reputation.

Further, there were causation issues. NT1 could not rely on harm that resulted from the legitimate processing of the information in the past (i.e. the threats that were made after the criminal trial). Some of the harm described, such as the impact on relationships, would have been as a consequence of the trial and conviction itself, and many people would have known about it from the reporting at that time, not from recent search results.

Warby J concluded that overall, the continued processing of information related to NT1's conviction and subsequent actions was justified according to the *Google Spain* criteria. Google's refusal to delist the information was upheld.

NT2 provided some witness evidence that supported his claims that the availability of the information related to his convictions on the internet had a '*profound adverse impact on [him] and his business and personal life, including on members of his close family and school-age children*'.[27] Whilst he too had not provided witness statements from his family members, Warby J, after hearing his evidence, came to the conclusion that it had gone '*beyond the evidence in the case of NT1*'[28] and had a stronger interference with his private life. NT2 had also provided credible evidence to show the adverse effect that the listings had on his business.

Warby J concluded that the information related to NT2's criminal conviction had become '*out of date, irrelevant and of no sufficient legitimate interest to users of Google Search to justify its continued availability*' and ordered delisting. However Google was not found to have failed to take reasonable care in the circumstances to comply with its data protection

---

27 Paragraph 216 (of the *NT1 & NT2* judgment).
28 Ibid., paragraph 218.

requirements, and therefore as per section 13(3) DPA 1998, it was not liable to pay damages.

GC and Others v Commission nationale de l'informatique et des libertés

In France, GC, AF, BH and ED each made requests to Google to delist results from its search engine displayed against their names. Google refused, and the individuals brought a complaint to France's data supervisory authority: the Commission nationale de l'informatique et des libertés ('CNIL'). The CNIL agreed with Google's decision. The applicants challenged the CNIL's decision in the Conseil d'Etat, which in turn joined the applications and referred them to the CJEU for a preliminary ruling. Some background to the applicant's erasure requests is helpful, to understand the context of the judgment.

GC requested delisting of a link to a YouTube video, which had been uploaded to the platform in February 2011. The video depicted a satirical photomontage that explicitly referred to an intimate relationship between herself and the mayor of a municipality, whilst she served as head of cabinet. At the time she requested the delisting she no longer held a political position.

AF requested delisting of links to an article in a daily newspaper written on 9 September 2008, which was about the suicide of a member of the Church of Scientology. AF was mentioned in his capacity as a public relations officer for that organisation. At the time he requested the delisting he was no longer employed by the Church of Scientology.

BH requested delisting of links to press articles about a judicial investigation in 1995 into the funding of the Parti républicaine, in which he was questioned with a number of businessmen and politicians. The proceedings against him were closed in February 2010. The links to the

articles were contemporaneous, and therefore did not mention the outcome of the proceedings.

ED requested delisting of links to two press articles reporting on a criminal hearing, after which he was sentenced to 7 years' imprisonment and
10 years' of supervision for sexual assaults on children under the age of
15.

The Ruling

Special categories of personal data

The first question was related to Article 8(1) and (5) of the Data Protection Directive. Article 8(1) covers the processing of personal data revealing racial or ethnic origin, political opinions, religious or philosophical
beliefs, trade-union membership, and the processing of data concerning
health or sex life. The equivalent in the GDPR is Article 9(1) that deals
with processing of personal data in the special categories (see Chapter
III). Both under the Data Protection Directive, and the GDPR, processing of such data is permitted where there is explicit consent of the
data subject, or where the data has been 'manifestly made public' by the
data subject.

Under Article 8(5) of the Data Protection Directive processing of data
relating to offences, criminal convictions or security measures is only
permitted '*under the control of official authority, or if suitable specific safeguards are provided under national law, subject to derogations which may
be granted by the Member State under national provisions providing suitable specific safeguards*'. The equivalent in the GDPR is found in Article
10.

The court was asked whether or not the provisions of Article 8(1) and
(5) must be interpreted as meaning that the prohibition or restrictions
relating to the processing of special categories of personal data, also ap-

ply to the search engine operator in the context of the processing it conducted in order to provide the search engine function to its users. It found that given the particular sensitivity of the data referred to, and that processing of it could constitute '*a particularly serious interference with the fundamental rights to privacy and the protection of personal data*', the provisions of Article 8(1) and (5) must also apply to search engine operators.[29]

According to the ruling, when the search engine operator receives a delisting request it must assess, with regard to the reasons of substantial public interest in Article 8(4) of the Data Protection Directive or GDPR Article 9(2)(g), whether the link to the information is necessary for exercising the right of freedom of information pursuant to Article 11 of the Charter.[30] Where the processing relates to the special categories of data, the interference could be particularly serious, and so it must be <u>strictly necessary</u> for protecting an internet user's right to Article 11 (my emphasis). The assessment takes place *ex post*, that is after a request for delisting has been received.

Consent and 'manifestly made public'

The CJEU discussed the question of whether or not a search engine operator could rely on the exceptions to the prohibition of processing special category personal data that were available in Article 8(2)(a) and (e) of the Data Protection Directive (GDPR Article 9(2)(a) and (e)). The court commented that it is '*scarcely conceivable*' that a search engine operator will seek the express consent of data subjects to process such personal data for the purposes of the search engine referencing.[31] By contrast, the fact that the data subject had made the personal data public

---

29 Ibid., paragraphs 44 to 48.
30 Ibid., paragraph 66.
31 Ibid., paragraph 62.

could be relied upon both by the search engine operator and the original publisher of the content.[32]

Offences, criminal convictions and accuracy

The CJEU clarified that information about legal proceedings brought against an individual is data relating to 'offences' and 'criminal convictions' within the meaning of Article 8(5) of the Data Protection Directive and GDPR Article 10, regardless of whether or not the individual was proved to have committed the offences.

However, bearing in mind the principles of data minimisation, accuracy and storage limitation,[33] and the judgment in *Google Spain*, a search engine operator must assess whether its links to webpages on information relating to criminal proceedings should remain, taking into account:[34]

> ➢ The nature and seriousness of the offence in question;

> ➢ The progress and the outcome of the proceedings;

> ➢ The time elapsed;

> ➢ The data subject's role in public life;

> ➢ The data subject's past conduct;

> ➢ The public's interest at the time of the request;

> ➢ The content and form of the publication;

> ➢ The consequences of publication for the data subject.

---

32 Ibid., paragraph 63.

33 Article 6(1)(c) to (e) of the Data Protection Directive, and GDPR Article 5(1) (c) to (e).

34 Paragraph 77 (of the *GC & others v the CNIL* judgment).

The CJEU added that even if the search engine operator did conclude that the continued listing of information related to legal proceedings was strictly necessary, it should adjust the search engine results in such a way that *the overall picture it gives the internet user reflects the current legal position*.[35]

Google LLC v CNIL

In 2015, the CNIL fined Google €100,000 for refusing to delist search results from all of its search engine's domain name extensions.[36] Google appealed to the Conseil d'État, which in turn asked the CJEU to provide a preliminary ruling on the extent of the extra-territorial scope of the right to be forgotten. The CNIL had been of the view that Google's proposal to use geo-blocking technology to prevent internet users from accessing results from other domain name extensions as insufficient.

By the time of the CJEU ruling, Google had made changes to its search service such that its users could no longer conduct searches on other domain name extensions. The user is now automatically directed to the national version of Google's search engine that corresponds to the user's location and displays results according to that location. Google argued that the CNIL's conclusion on global delisting *disregarded the principles of courtesy and non-interference recognised by public international law and disproportionately infringed the freedoms of expression, information, communication and the press guaranteed, in particular by Article 11 of the Charter*.[37]

The CJEU noted that Article 4(1)(a) of the Data Protection Directive and GDPR Article 3(1) permit data subjects to assert their right to delist their personal data against a search engine operator that has one or

---

35 Ibid., paragraph 78.
36 For example: .fr, .com, .co.uk
37 Paragraph 38 (of the Google v CNIL judgment).

more establishments in the EU, regardless of whether or not the processing takes place in the EU. *Google Spain* had settled the question of establishment in regard to Google's operations and had found it to be a controller for the purposes of the processing of personal data for its search engine (see Chapter IV).

Recital 10 of the Data Protection Directive, and recitals 10, 11 and 13 of the GDPR confirm that their objective is to guarantee a high level of protection of personal data throughout the EU. The CJEU recognised the global nature of the internet and that search engines make a search based on a person's name 'ubiquitous' and as such may have 'immediate and substantial' effects on a person in the EU.[38] It noted however that countries outside of the EU do not all recognise the right to be forgotten. The right to the protection of personal data must be balanced against other fundamental rights, in accordance with the principle of proportionality. That balance '*is likely to vary significantly around the world*' and the EU legislature has not '*struck such a balance as regards the scope of a de-referencing outside the Union*'.[39]

Whilst there is no legal obligation under EU law to delist globally, the CJEU pointed out that EU law also does not prohibit the practice and it was open to a search engine operator to do so. Further, a search engine operator must still take 'sufficiently effective measures' to meet all the legal requirements of delisting, which at the very least would involve '*seriously discouraging internet users in the Member States from gaining access to the links in question*'.[40]

---

38 Ibid., paragraph 56 and 57.
39 Ibid., paragraph 60 and 61.
40 Ibid., paragraph 70.

CHAPTER VIII
REMEDIES AND APPEALS

The primary remedy for a right to be forgotten request is that the personal data is erased or delisted. However, it is also possible to seek financial compensation. GDPR Article 82 provides for the right to compensation for any person who has suffered *'material or non-material damage as a result of an infringement of this Regulation'* and imposes liability on *'any controller involved in processing...for the damage caused by processing which infringes this Regulation'*. Note that the damage caused is not restricted to the data subject to whom the processing of the personal data relates.

GDPR recital 75 adds: *'the risk to the rights and freedoms of natural persons, of varying likelihood and severity, may result from personal data processing which could lead to physical, material or non-material damage'*. The recital lists the following in particular, where the data processing may cause:

➢ Discrimination;

➢ Identity theft and fraud;

➢ Financial loss;

➢ Damage to reputation;

➢ Loss of confidentiality of personal data protected by professional secrecy;

➢ Unauthorised reversal of pseudonymisation;

➢ Any other significant economic or social disadvantage.

Where a data subject is dissatisfied with a response from a controller, or wants to challenge a refusal notice, he or she may make a request to the ICO to investigate and take regulatory action or bring a claim in the civil courts against the controller. It is possible for the data subject to do both, and a response from the ICO is not required to initiate legal proceedings. The ICO may also decide to investigate of its own motion.

The ICO's main enforcement measures are:

> ➤ To issue an information notice requiring the controller, processor or other person to provide particular information requested;

> ➤ To issue an assessment notice against a controller or processor to enable the ICO to assess its data practices, which may involve entering premises, inspecting documents, observing processes and conducting interviews;

> ➤ To issue an enforcement notice against a controller or processor imposing certain requirements to correct the data protection failing;

> ➤ To issue a penalty notice against a controller or processor where it has failed, or is failing, to comply with its continuing obligations or with data subjects' rights, or for failing to comply with one of the notices listed above.

The GDPR brought data protection into the spotlight, in particular, because it substantially increased the penalties that a data supervisory authority could impose. It is possible for to fine an organisation up to 4% of its total annual worldwide turnover in the preceding financial year, or €20 million, whichever is greater, for breaching data protection principles and obligations.[1] Note that whilst the ICO may pursue the measures listed above, it will not order the controller or processor to pay the data subject financial compensation. Such a remedy can only be pursued in a civil claim. Where a controller or processor disagrees with the finding of the ICO, it may appeal against the ICO notices listed above to the First-tier Tribunal.

The Commissioner is obliged to take steps to respond to the complaint, investigate the complaint, inform the complainant of the outcome and provide the complainant with further information to pursue the complaint.[2] It is possible to apply to the First-tier Tribunal for an order requiring the ICO to progress the complaint if no appropriate action is taken within three months,[3] however in reality, it may be more direct for the data subject to pursue a private action against the controller in the civil courts.

A claim may be brought in either a county court or the High Court, depending on the usual principles. In general, the default position is that claims may not be brought in the High Court unless the value of the claim is more than £100,00, or there is particular complexity that warrants being heard by a specialist judge in the High Court.[4] Claimants must now follow the pre-action protocol for media and communications claims when pursuing a cause of action based on data protection if their case falls within the scope of CPR rule 53.1. The court can make compliance orders on similar terms to the ICO, that is, requiring the controller or processor to take specific steps (e.g. erase the data), and/or make an order for compensation to be paid to the claimant.

---

1   GDPR Article 83(5) for serious infringements such as of Articles 5,6,7,9, data subject rights and transfers of personal data. GDPR Article 83(4) covers less serious infringements, with a possible fine of up to 2% of annual worldwide turnover in the preceding financial year, or €10 million, whichever is greater.
2   GDPR Articles 57(1)(f) and 77(2).
3   Section 166 DPA 2018.
4   CPR PD7A paragraphs 2.1 and 2.4.

Until recently, a data protection claim could only be brought where there had been a resulting financial loss. The Court of Appeal in *Google v Vidal-Hall [2015] EWCA Civ 311* found that this requirement could not be read compatibly with Article 23 of the Data Protection Directive and it was struck down such that any damages – pecuniary and/or non-pecuniary – could be claimed under the DPA 1998.

A claimant may be compensated for 'material damage', which is financial loss or pecuniary loss, and also for 'non-material damage', which is a loss that is difficult to quantify, such as distress. The amount that a claimant may be awarded for 'non-material damage' can be difficult to assess and will depend on the particular circumstances of the case. There is as yet only a small body of case law on the quantification of damages in data protection. Most data protection cases have been brought alongside claims for defamation, misuse of private information or breach of confidence.

The amount that may be awarded for a failure to erase personal data will depend on the consequences to the data subject. Causation principles will apply. The claimant will need to prove on the balance of probabilities that the breach or failure has caused the damage or loss and that the loss was reasonably foreseeable. A claimant is unlikely to receive anything simply for the fact of a breach without any consequential effects, or harm, unless some economic interest is involved.

The quantification of loss of control of personal data and/or 'user damages' will soon be considered in the Supreme Court. On 11 March 2020 Google was granted permission to appeal against the decision of the Court of Appeal in *Richard Lloyd v Google LLC [2019] EWCA Civ 1599* which involved a claim related to the use of browser-generated information. The Supreme Court's decision will also be relevant on the question of group litigation (equivalent to US 'class action' lawsuits) in the context of data protection, which has been made easier since the GDPR came into force. The case of *Lloyd* involves around 4.4 million iPhone users in the UK, claiming £750 each.

There has not yet been a right to be forgotten case brought in the UK under the GDPR and it is therefore difficult to assess how the courts will quantify damages. The case of *NT1 & NT2 v Google LLC* was considered under the Data Protection Directive, which made a controller exempt from liability where it is proved that such care was taken '*as in all the circumstances [that] was reasonably required to comply with the requirement concerned'.*[5] Whilst NT2 was successful, he was not awarded damages, on the basis that the defence applied (see Chapter VII). The GDPR has narrowed this defence. The current position is that a controller or processor will not be liable for any damage caused by the processing of the personal data if '*it proves that it is not in any way responsible for the event giving rise to the damage*' (my emphasis).[6]

Given the paucity of reported data protection cases, in particular in relation to the right to be forgotten, it is not known how this type of defence will be interpreted, or causation generally. In particular, if the erasure request is brought on the basis of ground 4 – the personal data have been unlawfully processed – will damages be quantified on the consequential impact on the data subject from the unlawful processing, or the consequential impact of failing to erase the data when requested?

The list in GDPR recital 75 gives some indication of the types of non-material damage that could arise. Where the failure to erase the personal data has had an impact on the claimant that interferes with his or her Article 8 right under the Convention (see Chapter II), then privacy-type damages may be applicable.

---

5 Section 13(3) DPA 1998.
6 GDPR Article 82(3).

Examples of damages awards in data protection/privacy cases:

- *Gulati v MGN Ltd [2015] EWHC 1482 (Ch)* was a landmark decision on the quantum of privacy damages. Mann J made a number of awards ranging from £72,500 to £260,250, and created a 'layered' approach to quantum, that included an award for the 'loss of the right to control the use of private information'.

- *Campbell v Mirror Group Newspapers Ltd [2002] EWHC 499 (QB)*: £2,500 in damages for distress and hurt to feelings as a result of a photograph published in newspapers; £1,000 award in aggravated damages.

- *Mosley v News Group [2008] EWHC 1777 (QB)*: £60,000 for the mass publication of images revealing the claimant's sexual activities.

- *Cooper v Turrell [2011] EWHC 3269 (QB)*: £50,000 in libel, and £30,00 for misuse of private information for the disclosure of private medical information on the internet.

- *Ali and Aslam v Channel 5 [2019] EWCA Civ 677*: £10,000 to each claimant for causing 'real distress' by broadcasting footage of them in their bedclothes in a television show.

- *ZYC v Bloomberg [2019] EWHC 970 (QB)*: the claimant was awarded £25,000 for an article that revealed he was being investigated for criminal offences.

- *Halliday v Creation Consumer Finance Ltd [2013] EWCA Civ 333*: the claimant was awarded £750 for distress as a result of an incorrect record of a debt that was shared with a credit reference agency.

CHAPTER IX
BREXIT

The European Withdrawal Agreement came into effect on 1 February 2020 and the UK officially withdrew from the EU. The Agreement provided for a transition period, which will end on 31 December 2020, and after which it will no longer be possible to challenge UK legislation based on non-compliance with primary or secondary EU law. The Data Protection, Privacy and Electronic Communications (EU Exit) Regulations SI 419/2019 ('the Regulations') will come into effect at the end of the transition period.

The regulations create a 'UK_GDPR' and the GDPR will become the 'EU_GDPR'. The UK_GDPR makes hundreds of amendments to the EU_GDPR and to the DPA 2018. These are consolidated in two keeling schedules[1]: 'GDPR Keeling Schedule' and 'DPA 2018 Keeling Schedule' and will need to be referred to by practitioners at the end of withdrawal until there is a consolidating data protection act. The GDPR Keeling Schedule, at present, only amends Article 17 to remove reference to 'Union and Member State law'.

However, the European Union (Withdrawal) Act 2018 ('the Withdrawal Act') makes it possible for the UK to diverge from the GDPR in the future. Section 5(1) of the Withdrawal Act establishes that '*the principle of supremacy of EU law does not apply to any enactment or rule of law passed or made on or after exit day*' and further by section 5(4), the Charter will no longer be part of UK domestic law. Section 5(5) of the Withdrawal Act states that the disapplication of the Charter does not affect '*the retention in domestic law on or after exit day in accordance with this Act of any fundamental rights or principles which exist irrespective of*

---

1   A keeling schedule is an aid to understanding a bill that significantly amends an earlier Act. It is a schedule that reproduces the provisions of the earlier measure and shows the effects of the amendments.

the Charter'. And further, that references to the Charter in any case law, are to be read as references to any corresponding retained fundamental rights or principles.

Section 6 of the Withdrawal Act explains how a court or tribunal shall interpret retained EU law once the UK has exited the EU. Courts will not be bound by *'any principles laid down, or decisions made…by the European Court'* and *'cannot refer any matter to the European Court'* but may *'have regard for anything done on or after exit day by the European Court, another EU entity or the EU so far as it is relevant to any matter before the court*.[2] The Supreme Court or the High Court *'must apply the same test as it would apply in deciding whether to depart from its own case law'* when considering whether or not to depart from retained EU case law.[3]

The present government stated in its manifesto that it intended to amend the Human Rights Act 1998 ('HRA 1998'), which incorporates the rights in the Convention. The European Commission has made clear that Europe's envisaged partnership with the UK should be *'underpinned by commitments to respect for fundamental rights including adequate protection of personal data'* and that the partnership should *'provide for automatic suspension if the United Kingdom were to abrogate domestic law giving effect to the [Convention], thus making it impossible for individuals to invoke the rights under the [Convention] before the United Kingdom's courts'.*[4] Therefore the UK is likely to continue to be obliged to follow the jurisprudence of the ECtHR, which is substantially consistent with the *Google Spain* ruling. It is unclear however if the Convention will be able to make up for the shortfall in the removal of the Charter, in particular because the Convention does not have the

---

2   Section 6(1)(a) and (b) and section 6(2) of the Withdrawal Act.
3   Section 6(5) of the Withdrawal Act.
4   The Annex to the European Commission's 'Recommendation for a Council Decision authorising the opening of negotiations for a new partnership with the United Kingdom of Great Britain and Northern Ireland COM/2020/35 final,' 3 February 2020, paragraph 113.

equivalent to Article 8 of the Charter, namely a right to the protection of personal data (see Chapter II).

Whilst the HRA 1998 remains in force, under section 3, primary and subordinate legislation must be read and given effect in a way which is compatible with the Convention rights. Section 4 HRA 1998 permits a UK court to issue a declaration of incompatibility where it is satisfied that a provision is incompatible with a Convention right. Once such a declaration is made, the law remains in force until Parliament decides whether or not to amend it.

After the UK exits from the EU it will become a 'third country' for the purposes of the GDPR. The UK government is seeking an 'adequacy' decision from the European Commission. 'Adequacy' means that a third country has been found by the European Commission to provide an adequate level of protection of personal data such that data can flow freely between the third country and the EU, without the need for relying on the international data transfer mechanisms in GDPR Articles 46 and 47.

This is important for the UK, given the ongoing issues with some of the mechanisms. Recently, the CJEU decided that the 'EU-US Privacy Shield' – that permits the transfer of personal data between the European Union and the US – is invalid on the basis that EU citizens' fundamental rights were not adequately protected from US surveillance.[5]

When assessing adequacy the European Commission will take into account:

> ➤ The rule of law, respect for human rights and fundamental freedoms, relevant legislation, and access of public authorities to

---

5   *Data Protection Commissioner v Facebook Ireland Limited, Maximillian Schrems CJEU Case C-311/18*, 16 July 2020, ECLI:EU:C:2020:559.

personal data, case-law and effective and enforceable data subject rights;[6]

➤ The existence and effective functioning of one or more independent supervisory bodies with responsibility for ensuring and enforcing compliance with the data protection rules, including adequate enforcement powers;[7]

➤ The third country's international commitments, international organisations it has entered into, or other obligations from legally binding conventions or instruments as well as participation in multilateral systems, in particular in relation to the protection of personal data.[8]

Given these factors, it is unlikely that the UK will dilute its commitments to human rights standards, and any amendments to the HRA 1998 will need to adhere to the protection of individual rights and fundamental freedoms to be acceptable to the European Commission. In any event, controllers will still need to comply with the GDPR where their personal data processing falls within the criteria for territorial scope in Article 3 of the GDPR. UK data subjects will also be able to make an erasure request under the GDPR, if the controller falls within the territorial scope of GDPR Article 3, as well as relying on the equivalent rules under UK_GDPR.

---

6   GDPR Article 45(2)(a).
7   GDPR Article 45(2)(b).
8   GDPR Article 45(2)(c).

CHAPTER X
CONCLUSION

Since the *Google Spain* ruling in May 2014, Google has received almost a million requests to delist information, for more than 3.8 million URLs.[1] It is unknown how many erasure requests have been made to controllers since the introduction of the GDPR in the UK, but since the GDPR came into force, the ICO has received just over 74,500 data protection complaints.[2]

The complexity of the data ecosystem and the multiple actors and purposes in the processing of personal data has increased the concerns of individuals on how, why and where their data is being used. The right to be forgotten has strengthened data subject rights, incorporating both the right to erasure and the right to delisting. The success in making an erasure or delisting request depends on the specific context of the request, the grounds relied upon and the existence of competing interests.

There are challenges for both controllers and data subjects alike in the interpretation of the GDPR, and the application of privacy, data protection and human rights principles relevant to the assessment of the 'risks to fundamental rights and freedoms' which is a concept that runs throughout the GDPR. It is also uncertain how the UK will emerge after leaving the EU in the international data protection framework, and how the GDPR will apply in the UK. The only certainty is that the right to be forgotten will develop in time, and as technology evolves, it is likely to create both new problems and (hopefully) new solutions to how our personal data is used.

---

1   See Google's Transparency Report.
2   See the ICO's annual reports for 2018/2019 and 2019/2020.

MORE BOOKS BY
LAW BRIEF PUBLISHING

A selection of our other titles available now:-

'Covid-19, Homeworking and the Law – The Essential Guide to Employment and GDPR Issues' by Forbes Solicitors
'Covid-19, Force Majeure and Frustration of Contracts – The Essential Guide' by Keith Markham
'Covid-19 and Criminal Law – The Essential Guide' by Ramya Nagesh
'Covid-19 and Family Law in England and Wales – The Essential Guide' by Safda Mahmood
'Covid-19 and the Implications for Planning Law – The Essential Guide' by Bob Mc Geady & Meyric Lewis
'Covid-19, Residential Property, Equity Release and Enfranchisement – The Essential Guide' by Paul Sams and Louise Uphill
'Covid-19, Brexit and the Law of Commercial Leases – The Essential Guide' by Mark Shelton
'Covid-19 and the Law Relating to Food in the UK and Republic of Ireland – The Essential Guide' by Ian Thomas
'A Practical Guide to the General Data Protection Regulation (GDPR) – 2nd Edition' by Keith Markham
'Ellis on Credit Hire – Sixth Edition' by Aidan Ellis & Tim Kevan
'A Practical Guide to Working with Litigants in Person and McKenzie Friends in Family Cases' by Stuart Barlow
'Protecting Unregistered Brands: A Practical Guide to the Law of Passing Off' by Lorna Brazell
'A Practical Guide to Secondary Liability and Joint Enterprise Post-Jogee' by Joanne Cecil & James Mehigan

'A Practical Guide to the Pre-Action RTA Claims Protocol for Personal Injury Lawyers' by Antonia Ford

'A Practical Guide to Neighbour Disputes and the Law' by Alexander Walsh

'A Practical Guide to Forfeiture of Leases' by Mark Shelton

'A Practical Guide to Coercive Control for Legal Practitioners and Victims' by Rachel Horman

'A Practical Guide to Rights Over Airspace and Subsoil' by Daniel Gatty

'Tackling Disclosure in the Criminal Courts – A Practitioner's Guide' by Narita Bahra QC & Don Ramble

'A Practical Guide to the Law of Driverless Cars – Second Edition' by Alex Glassbrook, Emma Northey & Scarlett Milligan

'A Practical Guide to TOLATA Claims' by Greg Williams

'Artificial Intelligence – The Practical Legal Issues' by John Buyers

'A Practical Guide to the Law of Prescription in Scotland' by Andrew Foyle

'A Practical Guide to the Construction and Rectification of Wills and Trust Instruments' by Edward Hewitt

'A Practical Guide to the Law of Bullying and Harassment in the Workplace' by Philip Hyland

'How to Be a Freelance Solicitor: A Practical Guide to the SRA-Regulated Freelance Solicitor Model' by Paul Bennett

'A Practical Guide to Prison Injury Claims' by Malcolm Johnson

'A Practical Guide to the Small Claims Track' by Dominic Bright

'A Practical Guide to Advising Clients at the Police Station' by Colin Stephen McKeown-Beaumont

'A Practical Guide to Antisocial Behaviour Injunctions' by Iain Wightwick

'Practical Mediation: A Guide for Mediators, Advocates, Advisers, Lawyers, and Students in Civil, Commercial, Business, Property, Workplace, and Employment Cases' by Jonathan Dingle with John Sephton

'The Mini-Pupillage Workbook' by David Boyle

'A Practical Guide to Chronic Pain Claims' by Pankaj Madan
'A Practical Guide to Claims Arising from Fatal Accidents' by James Patience
'A Practical Guide to Subtle Brain Injury Claims' by Pankaj Madan

These books and more are available to order online direct from the publisher at www.lawbriefpublishing.com, where you can also read free sample chapters. For any queries, contact us on 0844 587 2383 or mail@lawbriefpublishing.com.

Our books are also usually in stock at www.amazon.co.uk with free next day delivery for Prime members, and at good legal bookshops such as Wildy & Sons.

We are regularly launching new books in our series of practical day-to-day practitioners' guides. Visit our website and join our free newsletter to be kept informed and to receive special offers, free chapters, etc.

You can also follow us on Twitter at www.twitter.com/lawbriefpub.

Lightning Source UK Ltd.
Milton Keynes UK
UKHW020635181120
373624UK00007B/869